Gardeners' World

THE COMPLETE BOOK OF
WATER GARDENS

Gardeners' World

THE COMPLETE BOOK OF
WATER GARDENS

Sue Fisher

BBC BOOKS

PICTURE CREDITS

BBC Books would like to thank the following for providing photographs and for permission to reproduce copyright material. While every effort has been made to trace and acknowledge all copyright holders, we would like to apologise should there have been any errors or omissions.

Boys Syndication pages 16–17 and 33; **Liz Eddison** page 65; **Sue Fisher** page 48; **Garden Picture Library** pages 8 9; (Duane Paul Design Team, photo Ron Sutherland), 12–13 (Gary Rogers), 28 (Mien Ruys, photo Ron Sutherland), 44 (Ron Sutherland), 49 (Chelsea, photo Ron Sutherland), 52–3 (J. S. Sira), 72 (Ron Sutherland), 76 (Gary Rogers), 80–1 (Lynne Brotchie), 89 (Denmans, W. Sussex, photo Brian Carter) and 120 (designed Henk Weijers, photo Gary Rogers); **John Glover** pages 61 and 77; **Jerry Harpur** pages 41 and 121; **Andrew Lawson** page 57; **London Aquatic Company** pages 92, 93, 96, 97, 100, 108, 109 (Bill Heritage) and 112; **Clive Nichols** pages 84–5; **Clay Perry** pages 24–5; **Harry Smith Collection** page 69; **Elizabeth Whiting and Associates** pages 1, 21, 37, 105, 113 and 116–17.

Published by BBC Books,
a division of BBC Enterprises Limited,
Woodlands, 80 Wood Lane
London W12 0TT

First published 1994
© Sue Fisher 1994
ISBN 0 563 36991 4

Illustrations by Will Giles and Sandra Pond

Set in Horley Old Style by Selwood Systems,
Midsomer Norton

Printed and bound in Great Britain by
Butler & Tanner Ltd, Frome and London
Colour separation by Technik Ltd,
Berkhamsted
Cover printed by Clays Ltd, St Ives PLC

CONTENTS

INTRODUCTION

WATER IS THE SINGLE most attractive feature that can be added to any garden. A water feature is enchanting and possesses a fascination that makes it a magnetic attraction for everyone, whatever form it may take. It lends the garden an air of peace and tranquillity, whether from the beauty of still water and the many reflections on its surface, or from the relaxing splash of a fountain or waterfall.

One of the advantages of incorporating water into your garden is that you can choose the form to suit the size and style of your plot, your budget and your enthusiasm. Water is versatile and adaptable, and features can range from a barrel pond or cobblestone fountain for the tiniest of town gardens or patios to a large pond and bog garden. A pond is also the most effective way of attracting wildlife, which is not only fascinating to watch but also beneficial to the gardener, as many of these creatures help control garden pests. A pond will also enable you to grow some magnificent aquatic plants.

The chief aim of this book is to de-mystify water gardening, making the construction and planting of a water feature as straightforward and attainable as possible for the ordinary gardener. The book describes ten different water features with detailed step-by-step instructions and diagrams showing exactly how to create them. A wide variety of features has been covered, so there will be something for just about every type of garden.

There are two major factors which can discourage the prospective water gardener: cost and the fear that a water feature will need lots of main-tenance. First, cost is an understandable concern, and it's true that larger features can be expensive, but with the aid of this book you can choose the feature to fit your budget. Each project contains a full list of the materials you will need, so that you can price it up accurately beforehand. The only other things you'll need are basic garden tools such as a wheelbarrow, spade, fork and rake. Remember that you can always extend your water feature at a later date – build the pond now and add a fountain later, for example. Second, the fear that a pond in particular will need a lot of maintenance and regular cleaning is largely unfounded: most of the work is in the construction, and a well-built and properly sited pond will require very little maintenance – one of the reasons why water gardening is relaxing!

The key to having a successful, trouble-free water feature is in the planning and construction. Before you decide which one to build, it's well worth reading Chapter 1, which is about choosing, siting and designing a water feature: it contains plenty of useful tips to make sure that you select the right one and site it properly. As well as the detailed information on water feature construction, there's a comprehensive chapter on plants to grow in and around your pond, concentrating on the more ornamental and less vigorous varieties which are best suited to the garden. Ornamental fish, however, are not covered in detail, though there are plenty of tips relating to the housing and care of fish throughout the book.

One word of caution before you begin. The instructions for constructing each water feature have been made as simple as possible, but do take account of the level of work involved. The simple sentence 'Dig out the excavation for the pond', for example, may not immediately convey the amount of physical work involved! But whether the work takes a few hours or a few days, you will get years of pleasure from your water feature.

CHOOSING A WATER FEATURE

ONCE YOU'VE DECIDED that you want a water feature in your garden, the temptation to rush out and start building it immediately can be overwhelming. But without some careful forward planning, you could be storing up all sorts of problems for the future. A water feature will have a high profile in your garden, it will take time and money to construct, and once built it cannot easily be moved. Rather than risk having an expensive mistake spoiling your enjoyment of the garden, take as much time as you feel is necessary over the planning stage.

Which Water Feature?

If you do not have a clear idea of what type of water feature to choose or where to site it in your garden, spend a little time clarifying your thoughts. The ten projects in this book cover a wide range of features, so there's a very good chance that at least one will be just right for you. If you already have a site in mind, this will influence the type and style of pond

Water is the focus of this densely-planted garden. Wooden decking gives the long pond a crisp finish, and the surrounding plants, such as bamboos and Fatsia japonica, *have lush foliage that is perfectly in keeping with water.*

you choose (see the sections on siting and designing below).

Carefully considering your requirements for a water feature will help make the decision easier. Here are just a few examples listed below of how assessing your priorities assists in choosing a feature and siting it correctly:

Your requirements	Tips to help you choose a water feature
Safety for young children	Cobblestone/millstone feature or wall fountain without surface water
Wildlife pond	Informal pond and bog garden constructed with a flexible liner
Moving water	Access to electricity is top priority
Water feature for a patio	Large patio – formal raised or sunken pond; small patio – cobblestone or wall feature

Cost usually plays a major part in the choice of a water feature. Obviously the larger the feature, the more the construction materials cost, but remember that you could always plan the layout of your feature so it could be extended later when finances allow. Do bear in mind that installing an electrical system and pump can add considerably to the cost.

Siting a Water Feature

Before looking at the aesthetic aspects of siting a pond, there are several practical points to consider. These may well rule out certain areas of your garden, and you'll find that this process of elimination helps in choosing the final site.

▷ A pond should get sun for most of the day. Shaded ponds will become slimy and unhealthy, and most aquatic plants need full sun in order to thrive.

▷ Ideally a pond should be sheltered from cold north and east winds so that the water temperature remains constant and therefore healthier for fish and other wildlife. Such shelter also benefits aquatic plants, as their young shoots are susceptible to wind damage in spring.

▷ Avoid siting it under overhanging trees or large shrubs: as well as shading the pond, they'll also deposit leaves into the water that will rot and give off gases that are toxic to the pond's inhabitants. Site the pond away from evergreens, the leaves of which are very toxic to fish and wildlife, especially yew, holly, rhododendron and laurel. The seeds of the laburnum tree are also poisonous.

▷ Proximity to large trees should also be avoided because of potential root damage. Rigid ponds are more susceptible to such damage than those made with flexible liners.

▷ Avoid siting a sunken pond in a water-logged site. This may sound odd, but a lot of water in the soil can press against the pond and distort its shape.

▷ Access to electricity should be borne in mind if moving water in any form is desired. From both the safety and cost aspects, it's better to run electricity cables for as short a distance as possible.

Designing a Water Feature

The ten water feature projects in this book are constructed to a range of designs, styles and materials, so there should be something for all tastes. But if you want to alter one of these designs or create a different one, here are a few useful points.

The siting and design of a pond should be thought of in relation to the garden as a whole, and the best approach is to do some planning on paper before you even pick up your spade. It's a good idea to measure your garden and draw up a plan to scale, so as to help see your proposed pond in perspective. Another useful way of doing this is to take plenty of photographs from all angles, including from upstairs windows.

Formal or Informal?

The siting of a pond in the garden greatly influences whether its design should be formal or informal. A formal design has straight lines, such as a square or rectangle or other geometric shape, and can be particularly suitable where space is limited. This type of design looks best in more formal surroundings, such as near the house, adjacent to the patio, or in conjunction with other features such as straight paths and paving. Ponds can be raised or sunken, but remember that a raised pond is very formal in appearance.

By contrast, an informal design is irregular, made up of soft, sweeping curves with few, if any, straight lines or sharp angles. This type of design looks perfect within a garden planted in a relaxed style. If lots of plants are your main preference, an informal style of pond is the best option – a bog garden can be created as an extension of the pond, and makes the perfect transition between pond and garden. An informal pond can be tailored to provide a wonderful wildlife environment too. To look as natural as possible, an informal pond should ideally be sited in the lowest part of the garden, where water would naturally be found.

Whatever your choice, beware of creating an over-complex design full of niches, nooks and crannies: this tends to look over-fussy and can be a serious challenge to construct! When in doubt, always err on the side of simplicity – ponds that are well-built to simple, straightforward designs tend to look far more attractive than awkward, complex shapes. A pond should also be at least 45cm (18in) deep at some point, to prevent the water freezing completely in winter.

STILL-WATER PROJECTS

A POND POSSESSES an indefinable charm and attraction that makes it a wonderful feature to incorporate in any garden. The beauty of creating a pond is that it can be made literally to any size and to fit in exactly with your requirements.

Marking out a Pond

Once you've decided on a design, the next step is to mark it out on the ground. Use pegs and string to mark out a formal shape, and a hosepipe or sand to mark out informal curves. Then stand back and view your potential pond from every angle and aspect – patio, kitchen and living room, as well as elsewhere in the garden. Look down on it from an upstairs window to get a clearer picture of the pond in the overall scheme of things. If you're not completely happy with it, leave the markers in place for several days so that you can keep coming back for another look. On no account start to prepare the site until you're absolutely satisfied with the design and siting of

This informal pond perfectly matches the style of the garden. Dense, attractive planting in and around the pond blends the margins with the garden and also provides an ideal environment for wildlife.

your pond: digging a large hole only to fill it in again will try anyone's patience!

Making Provision for Wildlife

Water in any form possesses a magnetic attraction for all forms of wildlife, from birds and hedgehogs to frogs. Even though attracting wildlife may not be your main object, it's definitely worth making some provision for their well-being – after all, these creatures eat many pests such as slugs, snails, aphids and leatherjackets.

The main priority is easy access. A steep-sided pond with a completely paved surround spells death for creatures that enter the pond and then cannot get out, for they will drown – even frogs and toads; and few sights are more pathetic than a drowned hedgehog. Just a few stones piled up to make a 'ladder' will avert such a tragedy. It's even better to create a 'green corridor' as well by grouping a few marginal plants together to sprawl over the edge of the pond. This provides good access for many creatures, and prevents tiny baby frogs and toads 'frying' on sun-baked paved edges.

Planning a Pond for Fish

If you just want a few ornamental fish, such as goldfish and shubunkins, there is no need to make any special provision for them, provided the pond is at least 45cm (18in) deep and contains a variety of aquatic plants. For larger species of fish a pond with a surface area of at least 4 square m (43 square ft) is recommended – equivalent to a pond measuring 2.4m × 1.8m (8 × 6ft). Small koi carp up to 20cm (8in) long can also live happily in a pond of this size. If you plan to keep larger koi carp, however, your pond will need to be designed specifically for their needs. It should be 0.9–1.2m (3–4ft) deep with a surface area of at least 7.4 square m (80 square ft), with a bottom drain to enable sediment to be removed. Few aquatic plants can withstand the vigorous attentions of koi carp, so in the absence of these natural water purifiers it's also necessary to install a filter to remove waste products and a pump to move water through the filter system.

Which Construction Material?

A pond can be constructed using one of three materials: a flexible liner, a pre-formed pond (also called a moulded pond or rigid liner) or concrete. Each of these is used in the first three pond projects described in the following pages, where their pros and cons are discussed fully. For the purposes of deciding which one to choose in the first instance, the advantages and disadvantages of each are briefly summarized below.

Flexible Liners

Flexible liners are sheets of material used to line a shaped cavity, which can be either raised or sunken. There are several different types of liner available.

Advantages
▷ Most inexpensive material for ponds
▷ Can be constructed to any size or design

▷ Good-quality liners are long-lasting
▷ A bog garden can be made as an extension to the pond
▷ Easy to transport

Disadvantages
▷ Can be damaged by rough handling and poor installation, or punctured by garden forks, etc.
▷ Cheaper liners can have a life of only a few years

Pre-formed Ponds

Pre-formed ponds are ready-formed shells that can be purchased in a wide variety of shapes and sizes, and in several different materials. Initially these can appear to be the most attractive option, but there are some drawbacks.

Advantages
▷ Good-quality ponds are reasonably tough and long-lasting
▷ The design is already done, so just choose the shape you like
▷ Can be used to install a pond on a sloping site

Disadvantages
▷ Good quality ponds are expensive compared with flexible liners
▷ The designs available may not suit your site
▷ Meticulous installation is required

▷ Some designs are too small or not deep enough to create a balanced pond environment
▷ Cheaper ponds are not very durable
▷ Difficult to transport

Concrete

Concrete has been largely replaced by flexible liners and pre-formed ponds, but it still has a useful role to play in certain situations. Consider making a concrete pond only if you're skilful at construction and have already done some concreting.

Advantages
▷ Extremely tough and long-lasting – a well-made pool should last a lifetime
▷ Useful if there is any likelihood of damage – for example, by animals or vandals
▷ Can be made to any size or design
▷ Can be temporarily filled in if necessary – for instance, while children are at the toddler stage

Disadvantages
▷ Time-consuming, costly and very hard work to construct
▷ Needs a reasonable level of skill, otherwise it could be a very expensive mistake
▷ Prone to subsidence damage after a long dry summer on some soils
▷ Should not be constructed during very hot, wet or frosty weather

A Pre-formed Pond

 Pre-formed ponds appear at first glance to be the most straight-forward way of creating a pond. Initially it appears to be temptingly easy – the designs have already been created, so just choose the one you prefer, dig a hole, put the pond shell in and fill with water. A pre-formed pond is particularly useful on a sloping site where the shell can be installed at ground level on one side and contained by a raised wall on the other; and it is also good if you want only a tiny pond. When it comes to anything larger, however, it's worth carefully considering the pros and cons of pre-formed ponds as opposed to flexible liners.

There are several drawbacks with a pre-formed pond. One that often isn't emphasized sufficiently in the sales blurb is that it needs meticulously careful installation. It's easy to forget just how much a body of water actually weighs: the water in our small featured pond alone, which measures approximately 1.5 × 0.6m (5 × 2ft), weighs around a

A pre-formed pond shell is ideal if you only want a small area of water in the garden. This compact little pond provides the centrepiece for a colourful display of cottagey flowers. The rim of the pond has been concealed with pieces of natural stone.

quarter of a tonne – the equivalent of ten large sacks of potatoes! So if the backfilling is not done properly, the pond can easily be placed under too much stress and become permanently damaged.

A proportion of pre-formed ponds available, especially older ones, are actually poorly designed and too shallow to house fish or wildlife safely, or indeed to create a balanced pond environment, so make sure that your pond is at least 45cm (18in) deep in one part. Material quality also affects ease of installation – cheaper materials are thinner and flexible, and therefore more difficult to install correctly.

There are several useful points to bear in mind when choosing a pre-formed pond. It's best to opt for a fairly simple, straightforward design. Some ponds are constructed with loads of niches and crannies, but remember that the more convoluted the shape, the harder it will be to install. A fairly recent introduction is pond designs that incorporate a 'marsh area' or pockets at the edges of the pond to contain moist soil. Some of these marsh areas, however, are too small or shallow to be effectively planted – the pockets should be at least 13cm (5in) deep. One option, if you want more input into creating your own design, is to purchase pre-formed modular units or sections, which are then screwed together. This does, however, make installation much more complex.

Pond size can be deceptive too. A pre-formed pond out of the ground looks enormous compared to how it will appear in your garden when only the top is visible, so be sure to buy one that's big enough. There is a wide range of designs available, and it is certainly worth obtaining several suppliers' catalogues and viewing a selection on sale before making your final choice.

Types of Material

Choosing a good-quality material is important if you want your pond to last for more than a few years. The rigidity and thickness of the material are indicators of the pond's durability and ease of installation.

PVC and **thin plastic** are cheapest but are least durable as they have poor resistance to physical damage, and to ultraviolet (UV) light which causes cracks and deterioration after a few years. The cheapest ponds are thin, very flexible and often have a simulated rock finish. They are mostly available only in smaller sizes.

Reinforced plastic is more durable and comes in a wider range of sizes, but again look carefully at the rigidity and thickness of this material.

Fibreglass is the strongest and best material available, and fibreglass ponds come in a wide range of sizes and designs. They are normally guaranteed for twenty years.

As with most things you get what you pay for, so it's best to invest in a pond of reasonable quality. If you decide to purchase a plastic or PVC pond, choose a dark colour, which is normally more resistant to UV light than paler material (see page 27).

Our pond measures approximately 1.5 × 0.6m (5 × 2ft) and has been used to introduce water into a corner of the garden along with colourful, informal planting. The edges of the pond are completely concealed by pieces of natural stone, and the plants tumbling around the pond help blend it further into the surrounding border.

Step-by-step Installation

1 Mark out the site for the pond. This can be easily done if the pond is a symmetrical shape by first turning the pre-formed pond upside-down and marking around its edges. Then mark out the site to be excavated 15cm (6in) further out on each side to allow sufficient space for backfilling. If your pond has a convoluted surface shape, don't bother marking out exactly – it's easier to dig an area such as a square or rectangle that contains your pond's design.

If your soil is sandy or crumbly, it may be necessary to slope the sides of the excavation gently. The important point is to leave a gap of 15cm (6in) round the sides and lip of the pond so that it can be successfully backfilled (*Diagram A*).

2 Dig out the cavity for the pond. Make the excavation 10cm (4in) deeper than the pond's actual depth to allow for a good padding of sand under the pond, and so that, when the edging stones have been laid, the pond rim will be completely concealed and the stones will be at ground level.

You Will Need

1 pre-formed pond

Pegs and string, or hosepipe, for marking out the site

Approximately 0.10 cubic m (3.5 cubic ft) sand to make a firm base (this is equivalent to 200kg in weight). If your soil is heavy clay or stony, extra sand will be needed to mix with the excavated soil for backfilling around the pond. In this case a total quantity of up to 0.25 cubic m (8.8 cubic ft) sand could be required.

To calculate quantities of sand for alternative base sizes, multiply the length and the width of the excavation together, and multiply the result by 5cm (2in), which is the thickness of the sand base

1 piece of timber (such as an 8 × 8cm (3 × 3in) fence post with the sharp corners removed) for tamping down the soil

Spirit level and plank (which should be just longer than the full length of the pond)

A few bricks to support the pond temporarily

Stone for edging

1 × 20kg bag mortar mix to secure the edging stones in place if desired. This will be sufficient for stones around 15cm (6in) wide; allow additional mortar for larger stones

---

If using just turf or plants to edge the pond, make the excavation only 5cm (2in) deeper than the actual pond (*Diagram A*). Remove a 15cm (6in) wide strip of turf from around the edge.

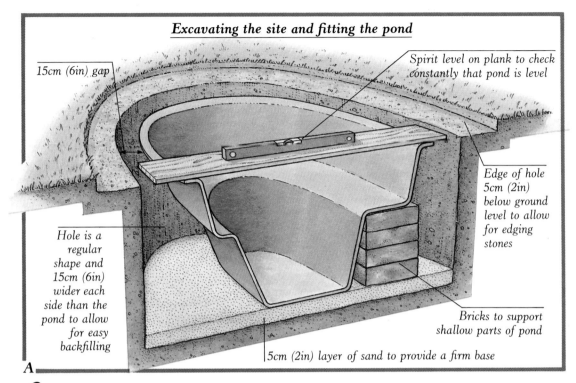

Excavating the site and fitting the pond

15cm (6in) gap

Spirit level on plank to check constantly that pond is level

Edge of hole 5cm (2in) below ground level to allow for edging stones

Hole is a regular shape and 15cm (6in) wider each side than the pond to allow for easy backfilling

Bricks to support shallow parts of pond

5cm (2in) layer of sand to provide a firm base

A

3 Use a spirit level on a plank to ensure that the excavation is level, both on the floor of the hole and at ground level. Tread the soil in the base of the hole firmly. If there are any loose, stony patches, take out the stones and pack the resulting hollow with sand. Go over the whole of the excavation carefully and clear any stones or sharp objects that could cause damage.

4 Spread a 5cm (2in) thick layer of sand on the floor of the hole to cushion the pond, stamping it down to make a firm base. Place the pond in the hole, supporting the shallower areas on bricks so that the pond is level (*Diagram A*). Check carefully with the spirit level to ensure that the pond is level on all sides, which is absolutely vital – a sloping pond will

leave part of the shell exposed and will stand out like a sore thumb! **Do not stand in the pond at any time.**

5 Prepare the excavated soil for back-filling around the pond. Check the soil quality and remove stones, debris and large clods of subsoil. If the soil is at all heavy or stony, mix in sufficient sand to make it a fine, manageable consistency that flows well. It's particularly important that the soil that will be close to or in contact with the pond shell is fine and free of potentially damaging debris.

Pre-formed ponds are available in many sizes, though installation of the larger ones can sometimes be difficult. The surrounding planting has been carefully planned to blend well with the pond.

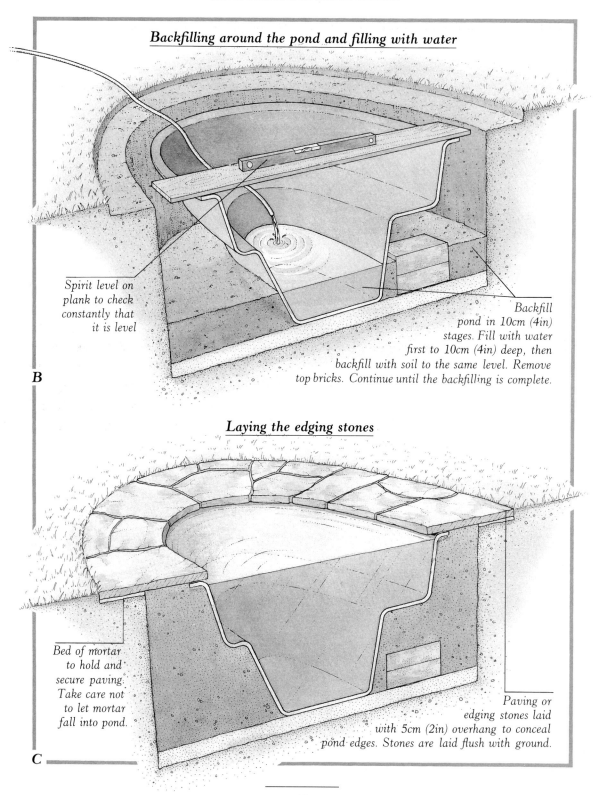

Backfilling around the pond and filling with water

Spirit level on plank to check constantly that it is level

Backfill pond in 10cm (4in) stages. Fill with water first to 10cm (4in) deep, then backfill with soil to the same level. Remove top bricks. Continue until the backfilling is complete.

B

Laying the edging stones

Bed of mortar to hold and secure paving. Take care not to let mortar fall into pond.

Paving or edging stones laid with 5cm (2in) overhang to conceal pond edges. Stones are laid flush with ground.

C

6 Fill the pond with about 10cm (4in) of water, then backfill with soil to the same level, using a trowel to pack the soil firmly underneath the shelves. Use the piece of timber to compact the soil firmly, though do be careful not to damage the pond in the process.

Check with the spirit level and plank that the pond is level. Don't continue any further until you're completely satisfied that the soil is closely packed and the pond is absolutely level (*Diagram B*).

7 Continue to backfill the pond in 10cm (4in) stages in this manner, adding water first and backfilling with soil to the same level. Pay particular attention to backfilling under the shelves – these are easy to overlook. Check with the spirit level each time that the pond is still level. Remove the top couple of bricks as soon as the pond can stay level unsupported

(*Diagram B*). The rest of the bricks can remain in the soil.

8 Once the backfilling is complete, lay the edging stones. These are best laid on a bed of mortar for maximum stability. Incorporate water with the mortar mix until it forms a stiff but workable mixture. Lay the mortar just outside the rim of the pond in a layer approximately 2.5cm (1in) thick and as wide as necessary, depending on the size of the stones. Lay the stones to project 5cm (2in) over the water, which helps conceal the pond material from view and protects it from sunlight – this is particularly important with plastic and PVC ponds (*Diagram C*).

Take care not to drop any mortar in the pond, as cement contains large quantities of lime that is harmful to fish and wildlife. If any does fall in, empty the pond and refill with fresh water.

PLANTING

A small pool needs plants that are correspondingly compact. Choose one or two of the small or compact water lilies on page 93 – Nymphaea 'Froebeli' is a particularly free-flowering water lily which bears deep blood-red flowers – or choose a changeable water lily such as N. 'Sioux' which opens soft yellow and develops to a pretty coppery-red.

1 or 2 water lilies
1 *Caltha palustris* (kingcup)
1 *Iris laevigata* 'Variegata'
1 *Preslia cervina* (water mint)
1 *Veronica beccabunga*
3 *Ceratophyllum*

Wildlife Pond and Bog Garden with a Flexible Liner

 Creating an informal sunken pond, especially one with a bog garden, is the best way to attract all sorts of wildlife into your garden. The activity in and around a pond provides an endless source of colour and fascination that will soon have you hooked. Birds come to the pond to drink and bathe. Frogs, toads and even newts take up residence, as well as many smaller water creatures. The aquatic and bog garden planting can be chosen to contain plants that attract bees and butterflies.

Our featured pond has been created to provide a perfect environment for all sorts of wildlife – the gently sloping cobble beach and the turf edging allow easy access for birds, and animals such as hedgehogs, to drink. Frogs and toads also love this type of edging as they can hop in and out of the water easily. A paved pool edge is not wildlife-friendly: access

Easy access to water is vital for wildlife. The cobbled edging of this pond is absolutely ideal for frogs, birds and other creatures.

24

Introducing Wildlife

Once your pond has been filled and planted, creatures such as toads, frogs, newts and insects tend to arrive of their own accord, often in a surprisingly short time. It's best not to introduce spawn from another pond, and it certainly should not be removed from ponds in the wild. Consider introducing spawn only from garden ponds containing excessive quantities of spawn within 1km (½ mile) to avoid disrupting the genetics of local populations, and to limit the spread of any disease.

Ornamental fish are best excluded from a wildlife pond, as they eat spawn and small creatures.

is extremely difficult for all creatures, and tiny baby frogs and toads dehydrate and die when trying to cross sun-baked slabs. A bog garden provides an excellent 'wildlife corridor' to a pond. The huge variety of plants in and around the pond attracts bees and butterflies, as well as providing an ideal home for many other different creatures.

The Benefits of Using a Liner

A flexible liner is ideal for constructing a wildlife pond as it enables the pond to be designed to suit the needs of all the different creatures and insects. The beauty of liners is their flexibility in more ways than one – you can construct a pond to whatever size or shape that you wish. Although this project is for a wildlife pond, liners can

also be used to construct a wide variety of ponds: raised or sunken, to a formal or informal design. A pond made with a flexible liner can also have an 'extension' in the form of a bog garden, where you can grow many superb plants that need permanently moist soil. These lush moisture-loving plants make the perfect transition from garden to pond.

A liner is also the most economic material to use for constructing a pond, and can be purchased in a wide range of sizes. A word of warning here, though – don't take economy to the extreme. There are several different types of flexible liner available, which all appear very similar at first glance apart from their price.

Which Liner?

The old adage 'You get what you pay for' is particularly relevant when choosing a pond liner. Quite simply, those at the cheaper end of the market aren't very durable and may last only a few years. When you're putting a lot of effort into constructing your pond, don't be tempted into a short-term saving by buying a cheap liner – it's well worth getting the best materials for the job if at all possible. It's also worth bearing in mind that cheaper liners have less flexibility and are therefore a little tricker to install. There are a number of materials available:

Butyl rubber is one of the best materials and has been used to construct ponds for many years. It is very tough, long-lasting and flexible, and can be obtained in almost any size. The standard thickness is 0.75mm (30 thousandths). It is usually guaranteed for up to twenty years.

EPDM (ethylene propylene diene terpolymer membrane) is sold under a variety of brand names. This material has only recently been introduced for pond use, though it has been used for years in applications such as roofing and inner tubes. It is extremely tough, but doesn't have quite as much flexibility as butyl.

LDPE (low-density polyethylene) is also sold under a variety of brand names. Normally there are several different grades available; the tougher grades are made up of several bonded layers and carry a guarantee of twelve to fifteen years. Lower grades are only a single thickness; they have a shorter life and are guaranteed for five to ten years.

PVC is also available as single and reinforced thicknesses and usually carries a five-to-ten-year guarantee. It can be up to half the price of a top-quality liner, but it is less durable. PVC liners are often available in several colours.

Polythene is the cheapest of all, but it is weak and therefore unsuitable for permanent ponds. It is, however, useful for lining a bog garden.

Deterioration of liners over the years is caused by the ultra-violet (UV) rays in sunlight. Better-quality liners have good UV resistance, whereas cheaper liners deteriorate rapidly. The most susceptible area is the part of the liner above the waterline which is exposed to sunlight, so protecting this part with a stone edging overhanging the pond by 5cm (2in), or concealing the edge with cobbles and plants, will help prolong the life of a cheaper liner. It also helps to choose a darker colour, as light colours are more subject to UV damage.

Calculating the Amount of Liner Required

It is actually very straightforward to calculate the dimensions of the liner, regardless of how convoluted the shape of your

You Will Need

(Materials and instructions refer to the pond only. Details for the bog garden are covered separately)

1 flexible liner
Protective material to line the cavity underneath the liner, the same size as above. Special liner underlay can be purchased or old carpet may be used, though the latter can be bulky and hard to lay. If you need more than one piece of material, allow an extra 10cm (4in) for every overlap
Pegs and string, or garden hose, for marking the outline
Spirit level and plank
Bricks or paving stones as temporary weights
Cobblestones to hold and conceal liner edges

Plants around this pond provide natural shelter for wildlife. Bees particularly like the pink Lythrum salicaria, *which contrasts vividly with red astilbes and yellow hemerocallis.*

pond either inside or outside. The formula to use is as follows:

Length = *maximum* overall length of pool plus twice the *maximum* depth.

Width = *maximum* overall width of pool, plus twice the *maximum* depth.

Add 15–30cm (6–12in) to both length and width to allow sufficient overlap at the edges. Where a pond has steep sides of 0–20 degrees to the vertical, a larger allowance is necessary (see Project 4: Building a Raised Pond, page 40).

Step-by-step Construction

1 Mark out the shape of the pond using string wound around pegs or a hosepipe.

2 Dig out the pond cavity just inside the markers. First excavate one half of the cavity to a depth of 30cm (1ft). Mark out an area 23cm (9in) in from the edges for the marginal shelves and slope the other half gently to the same depth. Dig out the central cavity to a depth of 60cm (2ft). The sides should slope at an angle of at least 20 degrees to the vertical to stop them crumbling; if your soil is sandy or crumbly, double this angle to make a gentler slope.

3 Outside the markers at ground level, remove the soil or turf to a depth of 5cm (2in) and a width of 45cm (18in). This will house the overlap of the liner and any edging materials. The markers can be removed once this has been done. Keep excavated topsoil separate from the poorer subsoil – topsoil can be used elsewhere, whereas the subsoil should be discarded.

4 Use a spirit level on a plank to ensure that the cavity, base and underwater shelves are all level. Make certain that the base and sides of the cavity are firm by pressing gently with your hands, otherwise subsidence may occur which can stress and damage the liner.

5 Once the cavity has been shaped correctly, go over it carefully with your

hands and remove sharp stones, roots or other debris that could puncture the liner. Line the cavity completely with underlay, allowing a 10cm (4in) overlap if more than one piece is used. This protective material is vital to prevent the liner being damaged by stones or other objects that may work through the soil in future.

6 Lay the liner loosely over the pond cavity with a roughly equal overlap on each side. Secure it temporarily by placing bricks or paving stones at the corners, but don't try stretching it taut – just let it lie loosely. If the weather is sunny, leave the liner stretched out for an hour or so to increase its pliability.

For this job and the following stage it's helpful to have two people to fit the liner.

Take great care that the liner doesn't become snagged or damaged at any time during handling. *Never stand on the liner*: sharp stones could easily have been picked up on the soles of your boots.

7 Begin running in water from a hose and slowly fill the pond – take plenty of time over this part. The increasing weight of the water will sink the liner to the deepest part of the pond and then mould it to the shape of the cavity. This is where you really need to be very watchful, moving the temporary weights, stretching the liner gently as it sinks, and

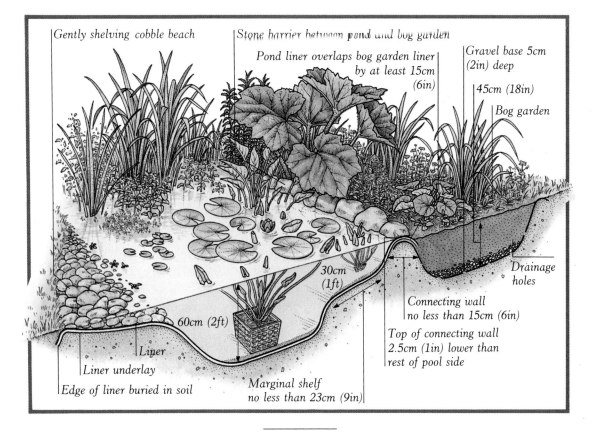

Gently shelving cobble beach

Stone barrier between pond and bog garden

Pond liner overlaps bog garden liner by at least 15cm (6in)

Gravel base 5cm (2in) deep

45cm (18in)

Bog garden

30cm (1ft)

Drainage holes

60cm (2ft)

Connecting wall no less than 15cm (6in)

Liner

Top of connecting wall 2.5cm (1in) lower than rest of pool side

Liner underlay

Edge of liner buried in soil

Marginal shelf no less than 23cm (9in)

ensuring that the overlap is still even – or you may find that you haven't got enough liner on one side at the finish.

Where the shape of the pond dictates that the liner will crease, such as at corners, pleat the surplus material carefully so that it makes a neat fold. In addition to these pleats, there will inevitably be a few small wrinkles, but don't worry too much: they won't show when the pool is complete.

8 Continue filling until the water level is about 5cm (2in) below the top of the pond. Trim any surplus liner to leave an overlap of 15cm (6in). Leave a rim of about 5cm (2in) width and bury the rest of the liner in the soil. Lay cobbles or turves to secure and conceal the edge of liner. If using paving stones, these should project over the pond by 5cm (2in).

Constructing a Bog Garden

A bog garden is created by lining an excavation with a waterproof membrane, and filling it with soil. This creates a pocket of marshy ground that is perfect for growing many beautiful moisture-loving plants. A bog garden can be constructed either as an extension to a pond or as a separate stand-alone feature, but either way it will need a regular supply of water to keep the soil moist; either from the pond or by hand from a hosepipe. Ideally a bog garden should be in a semi-shaded site, though a site in full sun is fine so long as there is no danger of the soil drying out. A bog garden adjacent to a pond should be constructed

You Will Need

1 flexible liner (see page 27 for how to calculate length and width). Either add these measurements on to the pond liner, or use a separate piece of cheaper liner. The quality of liner is not important, as the bog garden doesn't need to be completely airtight

Gravel for the base of the excavation

Stones or cobbles to form a barrier between bog garden and pond

Well-rotted manure, garden compost, or other moisture-retentive organic matter. This should be mixed 50/50 with good garden soil for filling the bog garden

at the same time as the pond, though it can be added at a later date with only a little extra work.

Old, leaking ponds that are no longer repairable can be turned into bog gardens. Simply follow the directions in step 4 below, filling the pond with prepared soil right to the top.

Step-by-step Construction

1 Mark out the area of the bog garden. Where the bog garden adjoins the pond, allow for a connecting wall of soil 15cm (6in) thick and 2.5cm (1in) lower than the rest of the pool edge. This will allow water to seep over from the pond.

2 Excavate just inside the markers to a depth of 45cm (18in). Check the cavity for sharp stones and other debris.

3 Mould the flexible liner to the shape of the cavity, ensuring that it fits snugly. Where the pond and bog garden meet, the pond liner should overlap the bog garden liner by at least 15cm (6in).

4 Make 1cm (½in) drainage holes in the side of the bog garden liner (except on the side where it meets the pond) at a rate of one every 1m (3ft). In periods of prolonged rain this prevents a build-up of water, which can become stagnant.

5 Cover the bottom of the bog garden with a 5cm (2in) layer of washed gravel. Fill with prepared soil to just below the connecting wall. Firm the soil gently, especially into the corners.

6 Build a layer of stones or cobbles on top of the connecting wall between bog garden and pond to retain the soil in the bog garden.

7 Top up the soil so that the edges of the bog garden liner are completely buried just under the surface. Fill the pond to the height of the cobblestone barrier so that water permeates through. Water the bog garden thoroughly and top up the soil if it settles below ground level. It is now ready for you to start planting.

PLANTING

Choice of plants is particularly important for a wildlife pond and bog garden. Ideally plants should be of some benefit to wildlife, and it's also important to get the right mix of plants to create a natural balance in the pool (see page 86) so that it needs very little maintenance.

Pond	Bog garden
1 *Nymphaea* 'James Brydon'	1 *Gunnera manicata*
1 *Nymphaea* 'Marliacea Albida'	3 *Mimulus luteus*
1 *Aponogeton distachyos* (water hawthorn)	1 *Sagittaria sagittifolia* (arrowhead)
1 *Myosotis scorfioides* (water forget-me-not)	3 *Veronica beccabunga* (brooklime)
3 *Caltha palustris* (kingcup)	1 *Iris pseudacorus* 'Variegatus'
1 *Menyanthes trifoliata* (bog bean)	3 *Ligularia* 'Greygnog Gold'
1 *Mentha aquatica* (water mint)	3 *Geum rivale* (water avens)
3 *Hottonia palustris* (water violet)	3 *Primula florindae*
3 *Ceratophyllum* (hornwort)	3 *Carex stricta* 'Bowles Golden'

PROJECT THREE

Making a Concrete Pond

Concrete used to be the only reliable material for constructing a pond, but it has now been largely superseded by good-quality flexible liners and pre-formed ponds, which are cheaper and much easier to install. The durability of concrete is its main attraction, and a well-made pond should last a lifetime. There are cases when concrete ponds can be the best option, such as if your pond will be in any danger of being damaged – if there's any likelihood of vandalism or dogs jumping in the pond, for example. A concrete pond can be made to any size or design, though it's best to stick to a very simple design for ease of construction.

There are several substantial drawbacks that should be carefully considered before deciding on a concrete pond. The materials needed are costly and the construction involves a good deal of hard physical work. A fair level of skill is needed too. A pond that is poorly prepared and constructed could deteriorate within a few short years and end up as an expensive white elephant, so don't even think of using this type of material if this is your first exploration into the joys of concreting! Concrete can also be a bad choice on a soil such as heavy clay that shrinks in prolonged periods of hot, dry weather, and can stress and fracture the concrete. Recent long dry summers have resulted in a number of ponds being damaged as a result of subsidence, and the only insurance here is first to line the excavation with a flexible pond liner.

Our concrete pond is constructed to a straightforward rectangular design measuring 1.8 x 1.2m (6 x 4ft). It is very much a permanent and central feature of this pretty, secluded terrace, which is screened from the rest of the garden by trees, shrubs and climbing roses. The planting illustrates how well the potentially severe lines of pond, paving and walls can be softened with a wide variety of plants.

Broadly the construction process involves digging a rectangular hole with vertical sides. A hardcore base is laid first, followed by a concrete base. Internal shuttering is then inserted and concrete poured between the shuttering and the vertical sides of the hole. Where soil is sandy or crumbly, however, it may not be possible to make a vertical wall in the soil without it collapsing. In this case external shuttering would also be needed. Because it would be supported by the soil, thinner shuttering with fewer supports would be adequate. Shuttering can be dispensed with completely in the case

A rectangle is one of the easiest pond shapes to construct using concrete, but don't consider this method unless you've already had some practice at concreting.

of larger ponds where the sides can be sloped at an angle of at least 45 degrees.

Colouring

Concrete can be coloured if desired, either by mixing coloured pigments with the dry ingredients prior to adding water, or by painting the whole pond once construction has been completed. Colouring is very much a matter of personal taste, and many people prefer plain concrete. Coloured paints normally available are natural stone, blue and black. The blue can look rather garish and gives the pond an artificial appearance. Black will give the best effect and look most natural. Always use a pond primer paint first, then apply two coats of coloured paint. To achieve good results, always follow the manufacturer's instructions carefully.

Options

You can purchase all the ingredients for concrete – sand, cement and gravel –

Note on Construction

Avoid laying concrete in very hot, wet or frosty weather. In hot weather the concrete will dry out fast, and if one batch dries before another is laid, these two batches will not seal together properly. Rain will affect the moisture content of the concrete, the correct amount of which is vital for an effective mix. If a frost occurs before the concrete is dry, it may cause weaknesses in the form of hairline cracks that could enlarge in future.

---

and mix them yourself. Hiring a cement mixer is definitely recommended, as opposed to mixing by hand. Pre-mixed bags of concrete can be purchased which have the ingredients already mixed, but this works out much more expensive.

For larger ponds it's worth investigating ready-mixed concrete from a specialist supplier, who will deliver mixed, wet concrete ready to be laid. Here it's best to enlist helpers to shift the concrete, as it will dry out fairly quickly. Once dry, it cannot be used at all.

Calculating the Amount of Concrete for Alternative Pond Sizes

First calculate the total volume of concrete required by working out the length and height of each separate wall and the base of the pond. Multiply length × height × width of each piece – the width is 10cm (4in) – then add the resulting figures together to give the total volume required. You'll then need to calculate how much sand, cement and aggregate will be required. The proportions of materials to use for concrete are 1 part cement: 2.5 parts sand: 4 parts coarse aggregate. At this ratio, to obtain approximately 0.17 cubic m (6 cubic ft) of concrete, you will need one 50kg (1cwt) bag of cement, 0.085 cubic m (3 cubic ft) of sand and 0.14 cubic m (5 cubic ft) of aggregate. Therefore divide your total volume of concrete by 0.17 (if working in metres) to enable you to calculate the amount of materials required. Allow an extra 10–20 per cent for wastage.

You Will Need

For a rectangular pond measuring 1.8 × 1.2m (6 × 4ft) × 45cm (18in) deep:

Pegs and string for marking out the site

Spirit level, and plank measuring a minimum of 2.1m (7ft)

For the shuttering, planed timber 2.5cm (1in) thick and 15cm (6in) wide; total length 18m (60ft), divided into six 1.8m (6ft) and six 1.2m (4ft) lengths

Timber for the upright posts, size 5 × 8cm (2 × 3in); total length 3.6m (12ft), divided into eight 45cm (18in) lengths

Timber posts for bracing the shuttering, size 8 × 2.5cm (3 × 1in); two 1.8m (6ft) lengths and two 1.2m (4ft) lengths

Several small pieces of wood for bracing the corners of the shuttering; four 45cm (18in) lengths of 2.5cm (1in) square wood are ideal

Timber spacers: approximately 12 pieces of wood 10cm (4in) long and 2.5cm (1in) square

Approximately 100 8-cm (3-in) nails

Tape measure, set square, hammer and saw

0.5 cubic m (18 cubic ft) hardcore for base

Powered mixer (optional but highly recommended)

For the concrete, 250kg (5cwt) cement, 0.43 cubic m (15 cubic ft) sand and 0.7 cubic m (25 cubic ft) coarse aggregate

5kg (11lb) waterproofing compound to mix in with the cement

Colouring (optional)

Shovel

Plasterer's trowel for laying the concrete

9m (30ft) long roll of wire mesh 60cm (2ft) wide for reinforcing the concrete. Maximum mesh size should be 5cm (2in)

1 wooden board, minimum 60cm (2ft) square to kneel on when working in the pond

Hessian sacking for protecting the finished pond until drying is complete

Sealant for treating the pond on completion

Waterproof paint (optional)

Paving to lay around the pond

Mortar mix to secure the paving slabs

Step-by-step Construction

1 Mark out a rectangle measuring 2 × 1.4m (6ft 7in × 4ft 7in). This is larger than the actual pond to allow for the thick concrete walls (*Diagram A*).

2 Dig out the pond cavity to a depth of 80cm (2ft 8in). Although the pond itself is 45cm (18in) deep, this extra depth allows for a 15cm (6in) thick hardcore base and 15cm (6in) of concrete base (*Diagram A*). The top of the concrete wall is 5cm (2in) below ground level to allow for the thickness of the paving slabs.

Keep the excavated subsoil and topsoil separate. The topsoil can be used again in the garden, while the subsoil should be discarded.

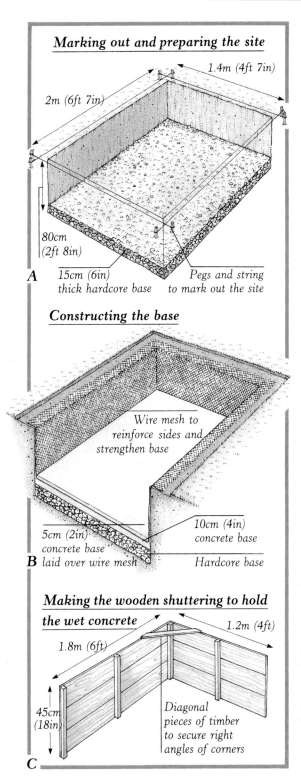

Marking out and preparing the site

1.4m (4ft 7in)

2m (6ft 7in)

80cm (2ft 8in)

A 15cm (6in) thick hardcore base

Pegs and string to mark out the site

Constructing the base

Wire mesh to reinforce sides and strengthen base

5cm (2in) concrete base laid over wire mesh

10cm (4in) concrete base

Hardcore base

B

Making the wooden shuttering to hold the wet concrete

1.2m (4ft)

1.8m (6ft)

45cm (18in)

Diagonal pieces of timber to secure right angles of corners

C

3 Use a spirit level on a plank to check that the surface of the excavation and the base are all level. Remove large stones and roots. Using a wooden post, tamp down the soil on the base of the pond to provide a firm base, checking afterwards that it is still reasonably level. Then lay a 15cm (6in) layer of hardcore on the floor of the pond, again pounding it firmly (*Diagram A*). It's important that the concrete is laid on a firm base, as this lessens the risk of subsidence and future damage.

4 The concrete base can now be prepared. This uses just over half the total materials, and it's best to mix the concrete in batches to avoid having surplus mixed concrete sitting around. Do not use concrete if it is already drying out. Note that the concrete walls aren't constructed until over twenty-four hours after the base has been laid.

5 First mix the waterproofing compound, which is purchased in powder form, into the dry cement at the rate of 1kg (2¼lb) waterproofer to 50kg (1cwt) cement. Then mix the dry ingredients of the concrete together, using a mix of 1 part cement: 2.5 parts sand: 4 parts gravel. Once these ingredients are well mixed and a uniform colour, slowly add water until the concrete is firm and workable but not runny. It's important to achieve the right consistency: you should be able to make ridges in the concrete with a spade which should hold their shape and neither slump nor crumble.

6 Attach a couple of pieces of string or similar material to the wall of the cavity 10cm (4in) up from the base of the pond to mark the correct level. Fill the whole base with concrete to this point, smoothing the surface with a plasterer's trowel (*Diagram B*). Use the spirit level to check that the base is level and even.

7 While the concrete is still wet, press the wire mesh gently into the wet concrete over the entire base and up the walls, allowing a minimum 5cm (2in) overlap wherever joins are necessary (*Diagram B*). This reinforces and strengthens the base and sides of the pond.

8 Then add a second layer of concrete 5cm (2in) thick to the base, over the wire mesh (*Diagram B*).

Concrete can be used to make a simple canal-like pond.

9 After three to four hours, when the concrete has just begun to harden, make a 'key' for the walls by roughening up a 10-cm- (4-in) wide strip of concrete around the border of the base, using a rake or stiff brush. This ensures that the base of the concrete walls will seal effectively with the base. Then leave the base to dry for twenty-four hours.

10 While the concrete is drying, prepare the shuttering. Construct the four separate shuttering panels by nailing the 15-cm- (6-in) wide timber on to the posts to form two panels measuring 1.8m (6ft) long and two panels measuring 1.2m (4ft) long. Both should be 45cm (18in) high.

(*Diagram C*). The panels should be smooth with no cracks between the timbers. Use the set square to ensure that the corners are at right angles.

11 Nail the four panels firmly together to form a rectangle, again using the set square to make certain that the corners are at right angles. Nail short pieces of timber diagonally across the top corners to ensure that the right angles are retained while the shuttering is inserted into the hole (*Diagram C*). So that the concrete doesn't adhere to the shuttering, spray the outside of the panels with water.

12 Lower the rectangle of shuttering into the hole and brace it with the four posts, so that the shuttering can withstand the pressure of the concrete from behind. There should be a 10-cm (4-in) gap between the shuttering and the walls of the pond (*Diagram D*).

13 The walls can now be constructed. It's a great help at this point to have someone standing in the pond cavity to hold the framework of shuttering in place to prevent it moving in the pond cavity while the filling is being done. Alternatively, use horizontal timber spacers between the soil and shuttering, removing them as filling progresses. Prepare and mix the concrete as described in step 5. Shovel in concrete to a depth of 8cm (3in) and tamp it down firmly using a wooden post to ensure that the concrete fills every niche and to drive out any

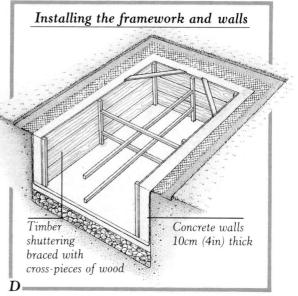

Installing the framework and walls

Timber shuttering braced with cross-pieces of wood

Concrete walls 10cm (4in) thick

D

air bubbles. Keep repeating the filling process until the concrete reaches the top of the shuttering, then smooth off the top of the wall (*Diagram D*).

14 Remove the shuttering carefully after three to four days.

15 The drying process normally takes one to two weeks. The concrete must dry slowly and thoroughly, otherwise hairline cracks may appear that could develop into larger cracks in future. To ensure that the concrete dries slowly and evenly, cover the entire area with damp hessian sacks once surface water has disappeared – usually an hour or so after laying the final concrete. Leave the hessian in place for one to two weeks, keeping it moist during that time.

If sacking is not available, spray the pond lightly with a very fine spray of water from a can or hose. Do this two or three times a day if the weather is hot and dry, but take care not to over-water.

16 The paving can now be laid around the pond. Prepare the mortar by adding water to the dry mix to achieve a firm but not runny consistency. The paving should overhang by 5cm (2in) all round the pond edge, to conceal the edges of the pond.

17 Once the concrete is completely dry, the pond must be painted with a sealant. This neutralizes and seals in the large amounts of lime contained in concrete, which is harmful to fish and wildlife. Unsealed concrete would result in lime dissolved in toxic quantities in the water. Sealants are normally purchased in granular form, mixed with water and painted on to the inside of the pond. Take care to follow the manufacturer's instructions, and paint the whole area thoroughly without leaving even the smallest part untreated.

A coloured waterproof paint can then be applied if a different finish is desired. Follow the manufacturer's instructions – usually one coat of pond primer and two coats of waterproof paint are required. In theory it should not be necessary to apply a sealant as well as waterproof paint. Some types of paint are microporous, however, and allow lime to seep through, so it's safer to apply both.

PLANTING

In a formal pond of this type which is a central feature, the planting needs to be carefully restricted. Here the aristocrats of the pool, water lilies, are the sole ornamental feature – choose two or three varieties from any of the compact or medium water lilies on pages 93–4.

Several plants with upright foliage would also make a good contrast to the straight lines of the pond.

1 Nymphaea 'Gonnêre'
1 Nymphaea 'Rose Arey'
1 Nymphaea odorata 'Rosea'
1 Acorus calamus 'Variegatus'
1 Iris laevigata 'Snowdrift'
1 Butomus umbellatus
1 Pontederia cordata
5 bunches of Lagarosiphon major

PROJECT FOUR

Building a Raised Pond

A raised pond makes a striking centrepiece for a formal part of the garden. Because of its formal style, a raised pond is usually best sited near the house or combined with a patio or seating area, where the sight and sound of water add luxuriance to a summer's day. A broad surrounding top to the pond makes a good impromptu seat or place to put down glasses and plates, and the nearness of the water makes it easy to view fish or other wildlife, especially for people who aren't very mobile. A particular benefit of a raised pond is that you don't have to dispose of a massive quantity of excavated soil when constructing it.

This design of pond tends to be quite costly because of the type and quantity of construction materials involved. For this reason, and also because of the high profile such a pond will have in your garden, advance planning is particularly important. It helps to achieve an overall appearance of harmony if you make the size of your pond echo a nearby feature – making it the same width as a nearby window, for example. Raised ponds tend to look best constructed to a straightforward formal design such as a square, rectangle or L-shape. When in doubt, keep your design simple: a well-built pond of a simple design tends to look much more effective than a complicated design, and straight lines are also far easier to build than complicated curves.

The bricks and coping stones should be chosen with particular care. Chances are they'll have to match your house and patio, so make sure that you don't create any colour clashes. It's well worth buying or borrowing a few different sample bricks to see how they look in your garden first – much as you would do with swatches of curtain fabric and wallpaper inside the house. Our raised pond is built using mellow old bricks constructed to a simple rectangular design. It makes an excellent centrepiece to this secluded leafy courtyard, and the pond materials perfectly complement the paved path. The ensuing abundance of straight lines is softened by a charming green carpet of *Helxine soleirolii* (mind-your-own-business).

This pond is actually only partly raised (see *Diagram A* for a cross-section of the pond). Because a pond should be at least 45cm (18in) deep at some point to prevent it freezing completely in winter, a smaller rectangle in the centre of the pond has been excavated below ground level. A part-raised pond is a good compromise that gives you the best of both worlds. If the pond were to be completely raised, the weight of the water would exert enormous pressure on the walls, necessitating a

A raised pond is a formal design and should be in keeping with its surroundings. This rectangular pond corresponds perfectly to the proportions of the courtyard garden.

You Will Need

For our featured pond which has a total pond structure measuring 3.68 × 2.3m (12ft × 7½ft):

String and pegs for marking out the site

Spirit level, plank measuring at least 4.2m (14ft) and builder's square for checking levels and right angles

Builder's trowel, small pointing trowel and wooden float for laying the bricks and concrete

300 standard size bricks (this allows a 5 per cent margin for any damaged bricks or bricks that need to be cut). If using expensive bricks, you can save money by constructing the inside wall with cheaper bricks.

For the concrete foundation, 150kg (3cwt) cement, 0.26 cubic m (9 cubic ft) sand and 0.42 cubic m (15 cubic ft) coarse aggregate

For clay, light or unstable soils, 0.4 cubic m (14 cubic ft) hardcore to provide a firm base for the concrete

For sandy or crumbly soils, 7.5 × 2.5cm (3 × 1in) timber planks, total length 5.8m (19ft), and about 1 dozen wooden pegs.

160kg mortar mix for laying the bricks and coping

Cement mixer (optional)

1 flexible liner 4.87 × 3.5m (16 × 11½ft) (see page 26 for information on choosing a liner)

Liner underlay of the same dimensions.

Coping stones 30cm (1ft) wide; total length required is 10.8m (36ft).

much stronger structure. The surround consists of three courses of bricks laid in a double wall on a concrete foundation. The structure is made watertight using a flexible liner, which is secured and concealed by the paved top.

Note that construction is done in stages over approximately two weeks to allow the concrete and mortar to set properly. This is actually an advantage, as it spreads the physical work rather than cramming it into a couple of days.

It's best not to start building your pond if there is any danger of frost, which can damage concrete and mortar before it sets, or if the weather is wet. Very hot weather also makes laying bricks more difficult, as the mortar will set quickly.

Concrete can be mixed by hand, but a powered mixer will save a lot of work and can be hired from tool hire shops. Cement, sand and coarse aggregate are readily available from builder's merchants and other sources. Bags of pre-mixed concrete can be purchased, but this is more expensive.

Mortar is best purchased as bags of pre-mixed material to ensure that the mix has the correct strength and proportions. If you want to mix the ingredients yourself, though, the proportions to use are 1 part cement: 1 part lime: 6 parts sand.

Calculating Materials for Alternative Pond Sizes

One standard individual brick measures 23 × 11.5 × 8cm (9 × 4.5 × 3in). These measurements allow for the layer of

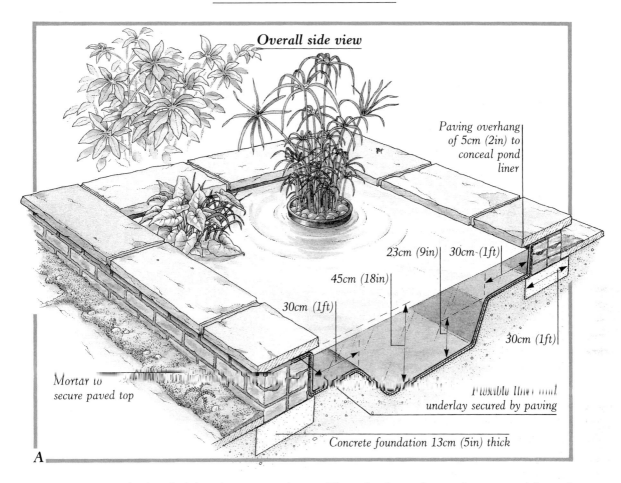

Overall side view

Paving overhang of 5cm (2in) to conceal pond liner

23cm (9in)

30cm (1ft)

45cm (18in)

30cm (1ft)

30cm (1ft)

Mortar to secure paved top

Flexible liner and underlay secured by paving

Concrete foundation 13cm (5in) thick

A

mortar around the brick. As a rough guide, 40kg of mortar mix will lay eighty standard-size bricks.

Calculate an alternative liner size as follows:

Length = maximum overall length plus twice the maximum depth.

Width = maximum overall width plus twice the maximum depth.

Add 60cm (2ft) to both length and width to allow for the steep sides and material for the overlap.

If the pond is a square or rectangle with no marginal shelves, tailor-made welded liners can be specially ordered.

To calculate alternative quantities of concrete, see page 34.

Step-by-step Construction

1 Use a spirit level to check that the site is level. Mark out a rectangle using pegs and string, measuring 3.73 × 2.38m (12ft 3in × 7ft 9in) – this is slightly larger than the pond, so the concrete foundation is wider than the wall for stability. Use a builder's square to check that the corners are exact right angles. You can purchase this, or make your own builder's square using three pieces of straight wood measuring 0.9m (3ft), 1.2m (4ft) and

A raised pond makes good use of a small area and, by using the same material for the paving and the pond, the sense of space is increased.

1.5m (5ft) respectively, which are nailed together (*Diagram B*).

2 Excavate a trench for the concrete foundation. Inside the string markers, dig out a trench approximately 13cm (5in) deep and 30cm (1ft) wide. Rake the base of the trench level, remove any debris and tread the soil firmly.

With clay, light or unstable soils, it's advisable to make a 15cm (6in) hardcore base to lessen the danger of subsidence. In this case the trench will need to be a total depth of 28cm (11in). If your soil is soft and crumbly, you may need to use shuttering – planks set on edge secured by wooden pegs – to retain the soil around the trench and contain the fresh concrete.

3 Prepare the concrete by thoroughly mixing the dry cement, sand and aggregate together. Add water gradually, mixing well until the material forms a workable consistency. Check this by making ridges with your spade in the concrete. They should hold their shape without either slumping or crumbling.

Fill the trench with concrete, using a piece of timber to push the concrete into all the corners. Level it off smoothly using a builder's trowel or wooden float, and check it is level. Leave for at least a week to harden. If shuttering has been used, remove it carefully after three to four days.

4 Once the concrete has set, the cavity below ground level can be excavated. Mark out a rectangle inside the foundation by leaving a 30-cm- (1-ft)-wide shelf all around the pond. Dig this smaller rectangle out to a depth of 23cm (9in), sloping the sides at around 20 degrees to the vertical so that the base is narrower than the top (*Diagram A*).

5 The brick wall can now be laid. Remember that the concrete foundation is slightly wider than the width of the wall for stability, so the wall will be built leaving approximately 2.5cm (1in) of foundation on either side. Move the marker lines in by 2.5cm (1in), and check that the corners are at right angles.

Prepare the mortar by adding water gradually to the dry material, mixing it thoroughly to achieve a stiff yet workable consistency — take care not to overdo the water. Mortar must be used within two hours, so it's best to mix small batches at a time.

6 Spread a layer of mortar 1cm (½in) thick on one corner of the foundation and lay the first brick firmly on it, checking it carefully with the spirit level to ensure that it's level, and making certain that it's parallel to the marker lines. 'Butter'

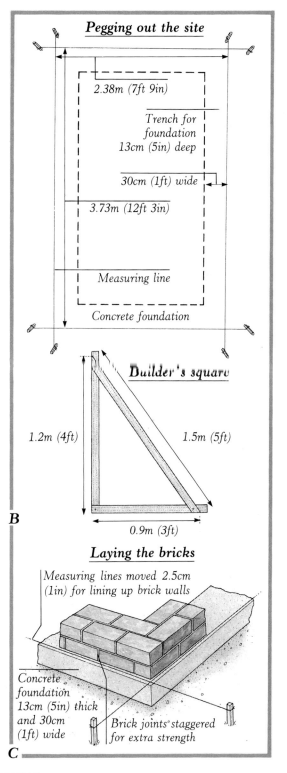

Pegging out the site

2.38m (7ft 9in)

Trench for
foundation
13cm (5in) deep

30cm (1ft) wide

3.73m (12ft 3in)

Measuring line

Concrete foundation

Builder's square

1.2m (4ft)   1.5m (5ft)

B

0.9m (3ft)

Laying the bricks

Measuring lines moved 2.5cm
(1in) for lining up brick walls

Concrete
foundation
13cm (5in) thick
and 30cm
(1ft) wide

Brick joints staggered
for extra strength

C

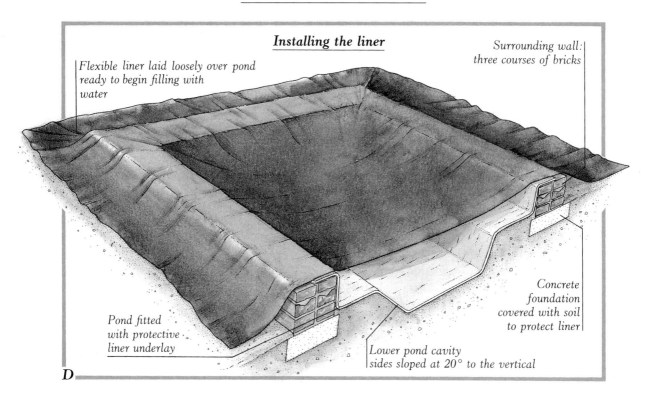

Installing the liner

Flexible liner laid loosely over pond ready to begin filling with water

Surrounding wall: three courses of bricks

Pond fitted with protective liner underlay

Lower pond cavity sides sloped at 20° to the vertical

Concrete foundation covered with soil to protect liner

D

the end of the brick with a layer of mortar and lay the next brick. Press the bricks gently but firmly together and scrape off any surplus mortar that oozes out.

7 Continue to lay the bricks as in *Diagram C*, finishing both courses of the first layer before starting on the next and checking all the time that the bricks are level and in line. Where the two courses of bricks are laid parallel to each other, make sure that there is a good layer of mortar between them. The layer of mortar between bricks should be 1cm (½in) thick.

8 Once the bricks have been laid and before the mortar sets, use a small pointing trowel to fill any remaining gaps with mortar, and smooth the mortar off to give a good even finish. Allow the mortar to harden for one to two days.

9 Check that the pond cavity is shaped correctly and go over it carefully with your hands to make sure that there are no sharp objects or stones in the sides which could pierce the liner. Check that the soil level of the marginal shelf covers the inside edge of the concrete foundation. Then line the whole pond with underlay, fitting it closely to the shape of the cavity (*Diagram D*).

10 To install the liner it's helpful to have at least two people. Take great care not to damage the liner at all times during handling – **never stand on the liner**, even when it's fitted in the pond.

Spread the liner loosely over the pond with an equal overlap on all sides, and begin slowly filling it with water. The increasing weight of the water should make the liner fit snugly into the corners, though it may need a little easing as the pond fills. Once the lower cavity is full of water, pleat the surplus liner material and fold it neatly into each corner, then continue filling. Stop filling the pond when the water is 5cm (2in) below the top of the wall, and pleat the liner again in the top corners. Once the liner is installed, trim off any surplus material to leave an overlap of 13cm (5in) to be secured under the paving.

11 Next lay the coping. Mix some mortar as before and use the builder's trowel to apply a good layer of mortar at least 1cm (½in) thick to the outside top half of the wall. Lay the paving firmly on the mortar so that the liner is secured by the inner edge of the slab. The paving should overhang the pond by around 5cm (2in) to protect the liner from sunlight and to conceal it from sight.

If you plan to install a fountain now or at a later stage, insert a piece of conduit (hollow plastic tubing through which the electric cable can be run) underneath the join between two paving slabs at the least noticeable point.

PLANTING

The planting here is slightly unusual in that the pots are a feature – normally marginal plants would be planted in special mesh containers placed just below the water's surface. The plants illustrated are Gunnera manicata, *with its giant rhubarb-like leaves;* Zantedeschia *(arum lilies) with bold heart-shaped leaves; and a tall* Cyperus *(umbrella grass). The plants illustrated are in terracotta pots and would need to be removed from the pond in winter and stood in a sheltered spot or an unheated greenhouse. If left in the pond, the pots would crack and the plant's roots would become frozen.*

1 *Nymphaea* 'Marliacea Chromatella'	3 *Iris ensata*
1 *Nymphaea* 'James Brydon'	1 *Glyceria maxima variegatus*
1 *Nymphaea* 'Gonnêre'	3 *Caltha palustris*
	8 bunches of *Lagarosiphon major*

PROJECT FIVE

Mini Ponds

 Miniature ponds have a charm and attraction all of their own, and one of the most attractive mini ponds can easily be created using a wooden half-barrel. The small scale of a barrel pond is perfectly in keeping as a central feature in a tiny garden, and in a larger garden it can be incorporated into a patio or seating area or just tucked into a border. A couple of marginal plants and a dwarf water lily can be grown in a tiny pond, or you could have a small fountain to give the relaxing splashing sound of water.

Opposite: Stone troughs are just one of many containers that can be used to make a delightful miniature raised pond. Even a tiny area of water such as this lends an air of tranquillity to a garden.

Below: A wooden half-barrel makes an excellent mini pond that looks good virtually anywhere in the garden.

Barrel ponds do have some limitations. They are unsuitable for fish to live in all year round because they contain a relatively small amount of water, which is therefore subject to a wide range of unhealthy temperature fluctuations. The water is also likely to freeze in winter, which would kill the fish. A good compromise would be to keep fish in a barrel pond from spring to autumn, provided it wasn't in a very sunny position. In winter transfer the fish, in water, to a frost-free greenhouse or a cool room indoors. Aquatic plants also benefit from protection in winter – either drain the mini-pond in late autumn and cover the plants with a thick layer of straw, or keep them in containers of water in an unheated greenhouse until spring.

Select a half-barrel that measures at least 60cm (2ft) across – this size should be readily obtainable from garden centres or other sources. Take care not to buy smaller wooden tubs that are made to look like half-barrels: they may not be strong enough or watertight. The condition of the barrel is important. All the wood must be sound, and the metal hoops on the outside should also be sound and close-fitting. Check the inside, and avoid any barrels that may have contained material such as tar, oil or oil-based substances that would pollute the water. New barrels treated with wood preservative are also best avoided for the same reason.

If you already have a barrel that you suspect is contaminated, you can still make it usable by lining it with a flexible liner. Secure this inside the barrel with wooden battens screwed on 5cm (2in) below the inside rim of the barrel, so that the liner doesn't appear above the water line. Unless the barrel is contaminated there is normally no need for lining, the only exception being if there are substantial gaps between the planks of the barrel – these tend to occur only if the metal hoops have broken or become loose. Don't worry about small cracks as these will be sealed when the wood becomes wet and swells.

There are many other containers that can be used either raised or sunken to make a miniature pond. Any container is suitable so long as it is waterproof and weatherproof – if the container is to be sunk in the ground and completely concealed, even a cheap plastic dustbin would do the job adequately. A wooden half-barrel could also be used above ground as a raised pond, though lining it with a flexible liner would be advisable to prevent any leaks. A miniature pond in a tub makes an unusual and attractive patio feature, and can usually contain two or three aquatic plants.

You Will Need

1 wooden half-barrel measuring approximately 60cm (2ft) across

Spirit level, and plank approximately 90cm (3ft) long

Gravel and cobbles to add the finishing touch

Step-by-step Installation

1 Thoroughly clean the inside of the barrel using a scrubbing brush and fresh water.

2 Now mark out the site for the barrel. This can easily be done by turning the barrel upside-down and marking out a square that completely encompasses its upper rim.

3 Measure the height of the barrel and dig out the hole. This should be 5cm (2in) *less* than the overall height in order that the rim of the barrel is just above ground level.

4 Firm and level the bottom of the excavation. Place the barrel in the hole and use the spirit level to check that it is level on all sides. Backfill around the barrel with soil and firm it into place. Fill the barrel with water.

5 Any planting in the soil around the barrel should then be carried out before the gravel and cobbles are put into place. This adds the finishing touch, setting off the pond and its planting to perfection.

PLANTING

The planting around a miniature pond is an integral part of the feature. Ornamental grasses and dwarf bamboos, such as the Arundinaria viridistriata *shown are perfectly in keeping with water.*
The evergreen Iris foetidissima *with its glossy green leaves is excellent for year-round interest. Leave the dead flower heads on, and in autumn they peel open to reveal glowing orange seeds. Hardy ferns, such as the* Phyllitis scolopendrium *(hart's tongue fern) shown in the photograph with tongues of fresh green foliage, are ideal next to water. Overall, the planting both in and around the pond has been chosen to provide a contrasting blend of foliage shapes and colours, from plants suited to this semi-shaded site.*

1 *Nymphaea pygmaea* 'Helvola'
1 *Houttuynia cordata* 'Chameleon'
1 *Eichornia crassipes* (water hyacinth)
2 bunches of *Ceratophyllum*

MOVING-WATER PROJECTS

ALTHOUGH A SMOOTH still pond is immensely attractive and relaxing, the rush of moving water exerts an absolute fascination and gives the atmosphere of your garden a completely different dimension. For those situations where a pond is not a feasible option, such as where space is very limited or where there are young children, a small moving water feature without surface water is the perfect solution.

It's hardly surprising that newcomers to water gardening, faced with an array of pumps, fountains, cherubs, dolphins and dozens of other accessories, can feel rather intimidated by the apparent complexity of achieving moving water. But like so many other aspects of water gardening, constructing basic moving water features is reasonably straightforward. The essential principle is that water from a pond or concealed reservoir is moved by an electrically powered pump, which is purchased as a sealed unit. Water is recirculated in the pond or reservoir, so

Moving water is both relaxing and dramatic, and there are an enormous variety of ways of including it in a garden. A raised rockery can easily house a waterfall which will bring the feature to life with movement, sound and light.

53

there is no need for a continuous water supply or drainage.

A pump also has practical applications, especially where fish are kept. Water circulating through a fountain or waterfall introduces life-giving oxygen to the pond during hot or humid weather and helps cool the water. A filter can be used in conjunction with a pump to remove the waste products of fish from the water, or to combat persistent green algae. There is more information on filters on page 70.

Projects 6 to 10 in this book show how you can achieve moving water with a variety of features. With an existing pond the simplest method of obtaining moving water is to install a fountain, which can be done simply by placing a pump fitted with a fountain jet into the water. If something more dramatic is required, a cascading waterfall makes a handsome feature. For an informal garden a small stream can be constructed in conjunction with a pond. A tiny cobblestone or millstone fountain provides the relaxing splash and burble of water beside a patio or as a centrepiece to a very small garden. For a town garden or patio a wall feature makes an elegant and attractive focal point. These projects provide a varied cross-section of moving water features. There are, however, many variations on the basic themes of fountains and waterfalls, should you decide to opt for a larger and more dramatic water feature.

If you're working on a budget, don't underestimate the cost of installing a pump. In addition to the pump itself, essential equipment such as extra cable, outside connectors and a residual current detector (RCD) all add to the final cost.

Types of Pump

There are two main types: submersible and surface pumps.

Submersible Pumps

Submersible pumps are suitable for the majority of garden water features, and are used in all five moving-water projects in this book. They have a vertical outlet pipe, which can be fitted with a fountain jet or connected to a pipe to convey the water elsewhere. An adjuster screw enables the water flow to be varied as desired. Many pumps contain or can be fitted with a T-piece. This will provide two water outlets to enable a waterfall as well as a fountain to be run from the same pump if desired. A small foam filter fits over the water inlet to keep debris out. Submersible pumps are easy to install and are quiet when operating.

Submersible pumps are powered in one of two ways. The majority operate direct from the 240-volt mains electrical supply, in which case the use of a residual current detector is highly recommended, to cut off the power immediately should any faults or damage occur. Alternatively there are low-voltage pumps which are connected to the mains electrical supply, and the power then runs through a small indoor transformer that reduces the voltage to a safe level of 24 volts. They are available only in smaller sizes.

Surface Pumps

Surface pumps are larger and more expensive, and are necessary only for larger or more complex water features than will be found in this book, such as a tall fountain, a high waterfall or several fountains, needing a throughput in excess of 4,500 (1,000 gallons) per hour. A surface pump needs to be housed in a specially built brick chamber, which must be dry, well ventilated and adjacent to the pond. When in operation the pump gives off a constant low humming sound.

Safety

Safety must be an absolute priority when installing and operating pumps and other electrically powered equipment out doors. It's vital to remember that water and electricity can be a fatal combination.

There are certain electrical standards for the components and wiring when connecting new systems to existing domestic electrical systems. In some countries these standards are mandatory; in others only advisory.

▷ Follow the manufacturer's instructions when installing any electrical devices.

▷ Use a 30-milliamp residual current detector when operating equipment directly from the mains electrical supply. This cuts off the electricity supply instantly should any faults occur.

▷ Use only equipment and fittings specifically designed for outdoor use. Use armoured electrical cable, or run waterproof cable through plastic conduit for extra protection. Bury the cable at least 45cm (18in) underground to avoid danger of damage by garden tools, and place markers above the ground to indicate its path. Alternatively run the cable under paving or along a wall out of harm's way. It's a good idea to make a clear drawing of the cable's position to pass on to any future residents of your house.

▷ The source of electricity is usually in a nearby house or outbuilding. The cable should come through the wall as close as possible to the pump. Where it passes through the wall, it should run through plastic conduit and be angled slightly lower outside than inside. Protective rubber or plastic grommets should be fitted to each end of the conduit to prevent any wear on the cable.

▷ If using a low-voltage pump and transformer which converts the electrical current to 24 volts, it's not necessary to use armoured cable or to protect the cable to the same degree, but do remember that the cable between the mains supply and the transformer carries the full 240 volts.

▷ The cable will need to come out of the ground near the water feature. Pumps are supplied complete with a length of cable, which runs out over the rim of the pond. This is joined to the power cable using a watertight or weatherproof connector.

The importance of taking sufficient care in using electricity in the garden cannot be stressed highly enough. When in any doubt whatsoever, call in a qualified electrician to carry out the work.

PROJECT SIX

A Simple Fountain

 A fountain in an existing pond is the easiest way of creating moving water. A submersible pump fitted with a fountain jet is simply placed in the pond, where it creates a beautiful sparkling fountain which can be turned on as desired.

General Tips on Pumps

There are many different sizes and makes of pumps on sale. To ensure that you purchase the correct pump for your feature it's necessary to have a clear idea of the functions your pump will need to perform, because its specific requirements will vary according to whether you want a fountain, waterfall or other feature, as well as according to its intended size. Each project contains specific points on choosing a pump for that particular purpose. There is also a number of general tips that are worth bearing in mind when purchasing any pump, as follows:

▷ Pumps carry technical information on their level of performance. However, this information relates to performance in optimum conditions and does not usually allow for the effect of fountain jets, length of delivery hose and other factors that reduce the rate of water flow.

▷ Within reason it's not a problem if your pump is more powerful than your feature requires. The water flow can be throttled down by as much as 50 per cent by means of an integral adjuster on the pump, and a more powerful pump simply gives a more gushing fountain or waterfall. A pump cannot be 'powered up', however, if it cannot cope with the size of feature.

▷ The flow rate of the pump needs to be in keeping with the volume of water in the pond or reservoir: for example, it's not feasible to have a pump with a flow rate that is greater than the volume of water contained in the pond or reservoir. The volume of water in the pond can easily be calculated by multiplying the pond's length × width × depth.

▷ Check the power consumption, particularly if the pump will be run for long periods. Some pumps are cheaper to buy than others but have high running costs.

▷ Check the manufacturer's guarantee. Most pumps carry a two-year guarantee, while some have a three-year one.

▷ Enquire whether the pump is repairable and check the availability of spares.

▷ Purchase your pump from a reputable retailer who is familiar with the range of products available.

▷ Establish the retailer's procedure if the pump breaks down while under guarantee. Many retailers replace your pump immediately, provided it has been

Creating a moving-water feature needn't be difficult. Just a simple submersible pump placed in a small pond will provide an attractive, sparkling fountain.

installed and used correctly. This is particularly important if you have a biological filter system.

▷ Enquire whether the retailer offers a pump exchange scheme should you mistakenly buy the wrong pump for your needs. Some retailers will exchange pumps returned in new condition within a set number of days.

Choosing a Fountain Pump

To calculate the correct size of pump for your fountain, you'll need to know the width and length of the pond so that the fountain spray doesn't fall outside the pond itself. To keep the feature in balance, the height of the fountain should be about half the width of the pond. If a tall fountain is desired, check the maximum head height of the pump – the 'head' is the maximum height to which a pump can move water and beyond which it cannot function. There needs to be a good margin between the maximum head and the height you wish the fountain to reach. In a more complex water garden where water may be pumped to a fountain from a lower pool, the head height is that of the fountain plus the height from the lower pool.

Fountain Accessories

The fountain head on your pump can be substituted with one of a variety of jets that produce different-shaped fountains. Check that the jet is compatible with your pump, as some jets are suitable only for larger, more powerful pumps. It's best to avoid jets that produce a very fine spray as this cannot be seen clearly and is easily wind-blown, leading to a significant drop in the pond water level. Choose a shape in keeping with your pond and its surroundings – a complex spiralling fountain would look a trifle strange in a small informal pond.

A more ornate type of fountain can easily be introduced by the use of a fountain ornament, the choice of which is totally dependent on personal taste and budget.

Installation is simple. Place the ornament in the pond, with plenty of padding underneath to protect liners or pre-formed ponds, or stand the ornament beside the pool. If standing the ornament in the pond, take care not to choose one which is heavier than the pond could support without being damaged. Place the submersible pump in the pond near the ornament, attach one end of the delivery hose to the jet which is ready-placed in the ornament, and the other to the pump outlet.

You Will Need

1 submersible pump

Either a residual current detector if the pump will be operating from the mains electrical supply or a transformer if using a low-voltage pump

Sufficient armoured cable, or cable plus conduit, to reach your power supply. (Note that pumps are usually supplied complete with several metres of cable)

Waterproof/weatherproof connector

1 brick or block of wood

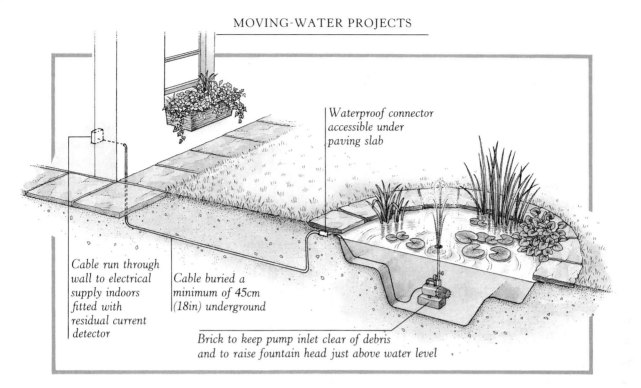

Waterproof connector accessible under paving slab

Cable run through wall to electrical supply indoors fitted with residual current detector

Cable buried a minimum of 45cm (18in) underground

Brick to keep pump inlet clear of debris and to raise fountain head just above water level

Step by step Installation

Follow local regulations for installing an outdoor electrical supply, which will generally be along the lines described below.

1 Mark out the proposed route of the cable to the nearest source of electricity – usually in the house. Fit a 13-amp three-pin plug to the end of the cable.

2 Drill a hole through the wall just large enough to allow the passage of the cable and conduit. The hole should be angled slightly lower outside. Fit rubber or plastic grommets to each end of the conduit to prevent any wear on the cable. Run the cable through the wall.

3 Dig a trench 45cm (18in) deep, which will place the cable out of the range of most garden tools. The trench should run to within around 60cm (2ft) of the pond. Lay the cable along the bottom of the trench. Alternatively run the cable under paving, along a wall, or in any site where it can't be damaged or trip up passers-by.

4 Use a special waterproof or weatherproof connector to join the cable from the pump to the main cable (follow local regulations as regards siting of the connector).

5 Place the pump in the pond on a brick or block of wood – this keeps the water inlet above the debris that naturally accumulates on the floor of the pond. The fountain head should be just above the water's surface. Run the cable over the rim of the pond, protecting and concealing it with slabs or stones.

PROJECT SEVEN

Constructing a Stream

 Few water features can invoke such spontaneous delight as a meandering babbling little stream. Such a feature doesn't grab the attention in the same way as a waterfall, neither does it possess the stylish elegance of a wall fountain. Instead a stream is a feature of subtle and captivating charm, something to stumble upon on a walk round the garden, much in the same way as you may come upon a little winding stream during a country walk.

There are few people fortunate enough to have a natural stream in their garden, but an artificial stream is reasonably straightforward to construct and makes a wonderful garden feature. A waterproof bed is made using a flexible liner or pre-formed sections, and the water is moved by a submersible pump placed in a pond. The layout can be varied considerably according to your own requirements and resources. A stream can connect two separate ponds, or the water can flow from a small 'spring' into the main pond, as in the photograph. A stream should be constructed on ground that is level or gently sloping. The sound of running water can be created by hollowing out the start of each section of stream to form small 'steps'. These should not be large, or there will be problems with excessive splashing of water.

The key to creating a successful stream is to make it look natural. By judicious use of rocks, pebbles and plants to conceal the construction material, the stream can be blended in perfectly with its surroundings. The design and layout need plenty of attention to attain this natural effect, so take enough time over your forward planning and marking out. Keep the design simple, both for effect and ease of construction: avoid straight lines or sharp corners in favour of gentle curves, and don't make the shape too convoluted or it will be difficult to construct. The shape of the stream bed and the water flow can be varied by placing

A stream is an ambitious undertaking, but the soothing babble of running water certainly makes it worth the effort.

Pump Maintenance

Submersible pumps need little maintenance. The filter should be removed and rinsed in clean water to get rid of any accumulated debris. Fortnightly to monthly cleaning is usually sufficient, but it becomes very obvious when this is needed, as the water flow through the fountain starts to reduce. In autumn it's best to remove the pump at the point where the cables are joined by the outside connector, in order to clean and store it over winter according to the manufacturer's instructions. Remember to protect the connector and disconnect the mains supply.

You Will Need

(Materials and construction details apply to the construction of the stream only and do not include the pond. For details of how to construct a similar pond, see Project 3)

For a stream measuring 3.6m (12ft) long, 45cm (18in) wide and 15cm (6in) deep:

Pegs and string, or hosepipe, for marking out the site

Spirit level

Flexible liner measuring 1.2 × 5m (4 × 16½ft) for the stream itself. Depending on your source of supply, it may be possible to purchase the liner only in several pieces. If so, add an additional 30cm (1ft) to the length of each piece to allow adequate overlap

Liner underlay, the same size as the liner

Gravel and small cobbles to conceal the stream bed

Larger rocks and cobbles for the stream bed and to conceal the stream edges

1 submersible pump

1 brick or block of wood

Sufficient armoured cable or cable plus conduit to reach the power source

Either a residual current detector if using a mains-voltage pump or a transformer if using a low-voltage pump

Waterproof/weatherproof connector

Minimum 4.8m (16ft) of delivery hose. Allow extra if the hose is to be buried or laid in a less direct route

rocks in the stream, as in the photograph, rather than by shaping it over-much at the construction stage. A good design option is to curve the stream rather than running it in an approximate straight line, as this shortens the amount of delivery hose required and therefore minimizes the size of pump needed.

Our featured stream has been constructed using a flexible liner. The water bubbles down a stream bed lined with rocks and gravel, and surrounded by lush waterside plants, into a large pond. This pond has also been constructed using a flexible liner to an informal design, with a sloping cobble beach and aquatic plants to disguise the pond's edges. The submersible pump is placed in the pond near the end of the stream and delivers water back to the start via a concealed hose. Here the water looks as though it rises naturally in a stone-filled basin, just out of sight in the bottom of the photograph.

The two principal materials from which to choose for constructing a stream are a flexible liner and a pre-formed unit. A liner is best as it enables you to create a stream of any size or design, and with a little care in the design and finishing it looks most natural. A pre-formed unit is a little easier to install but is more difficult to conceal. Such a unit is sold in sections, which does allow some flexibility in the design but nowhere near as much as with a liner. The important point to remember when installing a pre-formed unit is that the front lip of one section is designed to rest on the back edge of the lower section.

If a larger gap is created, there will be problems with excessive splashing.

Whatever your materials, it's well worth buying the best quality you can afford rather than choosing cheaper materials that can have a limited life. See pages 18 and 26 for more details on different types of material.

Choosing a Pump for a Stream

There are general details on choosing a pump on page 56, which it's advisable to read first.

A pump for any sort of stream will need to be fairly powerful in order to achieve an adequate flow rate. The head height of the pump, however, is minimal by comparison.

IMPORTANT: **Read the safety notes and general information on pumps on page 55 before buying and installing a pump and fittings.**

Step-by-step Construction

1 Mark out the path of the stream using pegs and string, or a hosepipe.

2 Starting at the pond end and working upwards, dig out the stream bed to form a shallow basin 45cm (18in) wide, 15cm (6in) deep and 1.2m (4ft) long (*Diagram B*). The stream should be shaped carefully, with each part of the stream bed running on an extremely gentle gradient of around 1 in 100. Each section of stream should be approximately 5–7.5cm (2–3in)

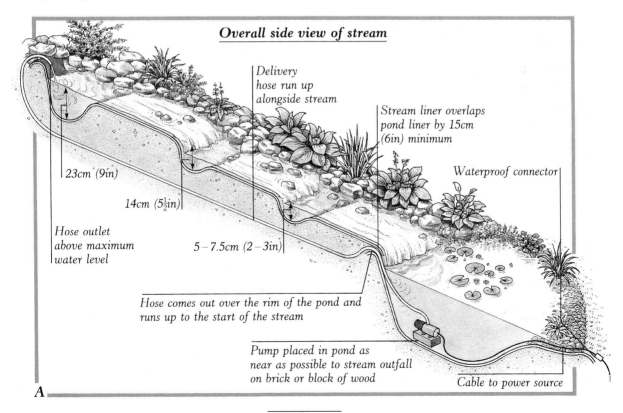

Overall side view of stream

Delivery hose run up alongside stream

Stream liner overlaps pond liner by 15cm (6in) minimum

Waterproof connector

23cm (9in)

14cm (5½in)

Hose outlet above maximum water level

5 – 7.5cm (2–3in)

Hose comes out over the rim of the pond and runs up to the start of the stream

Pump placed in pond as near as possible to stream outfall on brick or block of wood

Cable to power source

A

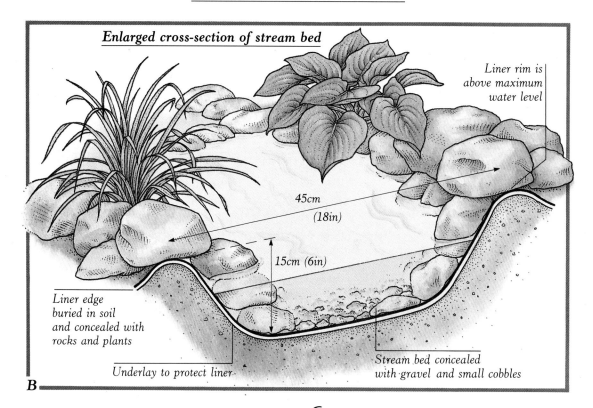

Enlarged cross-section of stream bed

Liner rim is above maximum water level

45cm (18in)

15cm (6in)

Liner edge buried in soil and concealed with rocks and plants

Underlay to protect liner

Stream bed concealed with gravel and small cobbles

B

above the lower one (*Diagram A*). The length of each section can be varied according to the size and overall layout.

3 Where the 'steps' of each section join, excavate the start of each section to form a shallow basin 5–7.5cm (3in) lower than the stream bed. This will create the sound of splashing water.

4 Excavate a basin 23cm (9in) deep to provide a small header pool at the very start of the stream (*Diagram A*).

5 Use the spirit level to check that the opposite banks of each section are level. Check carefully that the pool and stream bed are shaped correctly, because this is vital to the success of the feature.

6 Go over the excavation very carefully, removing any stones or sharp objects that could damage the liner. Fit liner underlay into the stream bed.

7 Again starting at the bottom of the stream nearest the pond, place the liner in position, smoothing it carefully to fit the contours of the excavation. Allow an overlap of 15cm (6in) where the stream

An unusual edging of woven willow adds to the charm of this informal wildlife garden. Such an edging could be used to retain the bank of a natural stream, or to conceal the lining material of an artificial stream. The planting in the grass makes a glorious spring picture – cream and yellow daffodils, buttercups, and Trollius (globe flowers).

joins the main pool and where pieces of liner overlap – the overlap should always be in the direction the water flows (*Diagram A*).

8 Once the liner is fitted to your satisfaction, leave a rim 5cm (2in) wide and bury the edges of the liner in the soil, ensuring that the liner rim is above the maximum water level (*Diagram B*).

9 Install the electrical supply and pump as detailed in steps 1–4 on page 59.

10 Place the pump in the pond on a brick or block of wood as near as possible to the end of the stream to minimize the length of the delivery hose. Attach one end of the hose to the pump outlet and run it up beside the stream (*Diagram A*). Make sure that the hose is not kinked or trapped, then switch the pump on. If the flow rate is insufficient to produce a reasonable stream and is substantially less than the pump's rated flow, the pressure loss along the length of the hose may be throttling the pump outflow, in which case a larger-diameter hose should be used.

11 Conceal the hose with stones and plants. Alternatively bury the hose out of sight, but remember to allow for extra hose in this case.

12 Position the end of the hose at the start of the stream (*Diagram A*). Fill or edge the header basin with washed cobbles and conceal the end of the hose as much as possible. Ensure that the end is above maximum water level or water could be siphoned back down when the pump is turned off.

13 Before placing stones or gravel in the stream, wash them with a hose to remove dust and debris. Then place rocks along the sides of the stream and pool to conceal the liner, taking care that there are no sharp edges in contact with the liner. Place rocks, small cobbles and gravel along the bed of the stream to create a natural appearance.

Shrubs to associate with streams and ponds

Aquatic plants all die back in winter, so it's worth including some attractive shrubs in the planting around your pond. Those with coloured stems look wonderful, particularly as the colour is reflected on the water's surface. *Cornus* varieties (dogwoods) are ideal garden plants that also have attractive foliage – *C. alba* 'Aurea' has beautiful golden leaves, and those of *C.a.* 'Elegantissima' and *C.a.* 'Sibirica Variegata' are green and white. In autumn the leaves fall to reveal glowing red stems. *C. sanguinea* 'Winter Flame' has fiery orange stems, as does *Salix alba* 'Britzensis'. Prune them hard every spring to encourage new, colourful shoots.

Evergreens provide good year-round structure and colourful foliage that comes into its own in wintertime. Plant evergreens well back from the water's edge, however, as the leaves can be toxic if allowed to rot in the pond.

PLANTING

For a natural-looking feature such as a stream, the planting plays a particularly important role in blending the stream in with the surrounding garden and concealing any artificial appearance the construction may have. Alongside our featured stream the planting has achieved this object — clumps of herbaceous perennials and ornamental grasses have been combined informally to good effect, with a range of foliage shapes and colours that look good from spring to autumn. These plants also associate well with water, and are planted right up to the water's edge to help disguise the artificial appearance of the stream itself.

The optimum soil for streamside planting is one which is moisture-retentive, to enable bog plants to be grown. One option on drier soils is to create a bog garden (see page 30). Another alternative is to incorporate plenty of organic matter such as well-rotted manure or compost, to increase the moisture-holding capacity of the soil, and to grow plants such as ornamental grasses, bamboos, hostas, and herbaceous perennials with bold, arching or feathery foliage that associates well with water. A number of suitable plants are described in the section on plants to associate with ponds on page 112.

Plants to edge a stream.
(Note: these plants are suitable for a soil that retains moisture through the year).
1 Carex stricta 'Bowles Golden'
3 Astilbe simplicifolia 'Sprite'
3 Hosta crispula
3 Hosta sieboldiana 'Elegans'
3 Geum rivale
1 Ligularia 'Desdemona'
5 Primula denticulata
1 Rodgersia aesculifolia
3 Ajuga reptans 'Purpurea'
3 Alchemilla mollis
1 Hakonochloa macra 'Aureola'
3 Imperator cylindrica 'Red Baron'
1 Sambucus racemosa 'Tenuifolia'
3 Primula florindae

Making a Waterfall

 Water tumbling down the steps of a waterfall creates a feature that is dramatic, both visually and audibly. Obviously there is more work involved in the construction than with a fountain, but a waterfall need not be large or grandiose – just two or three 'steps' will give a very attractive effect. As with most features, a waterfall can be as simple or as complex as you wish.

Unless you're fortunate enough to have a natural slope or mound in just the right place, you will need to construct one in order to provide the necessary height for the waterfall. The height needn't be great – 60–90cm (2–3ft) is ample to provide an effective waterfall – but careful planning is necessary before construction begins. A waterfall must be planned and designed either to look very natural and informal, blended in to the mound with rocks and planting, or it must be obviously formal with straight channels. The style of waterfall should match the style of pond: a meandering informal waterfall would look out of place with a formal pond, for example, and vice versa. Access to electricity for the pump is an essential consideration.

Our waterfall uses a variety of contrasting materials for maximum effect. The watercourse is created using attractive, weathered paving slabs to form the steps; the rigid lines of the sides are broken up with pieces of natural stone and softened by planting. The 'steps' are made watertight by the use of a flexible liner – one of good quality is definitely recommended. The waterfall as a whole must be completely watertight: as water is constantly circulating from the pond, any leaks would result in continuous water loss. The stone and plants also conceal the delivery hose that circulates water from the pond to the top of the fall, and the water tumbles down to the shallow edge which is lined with cobbles. The overall height of the waterfall is 90cm (3ft).

Construction Materials

There are two main materials to use for a waterfall: pre-formed units or a flexible liner. Concrete can be used but is not recommended unless you're skilled in its use. In any case, it's best to line a concrete waterfall with a flexible liner as an additional precaution against seepages.

Pre-formed Units

Pre-formed units are by far the easiest method of waterfall construction, but can look most artificial. Units come in a whole variety of shapes, sizes and finishes. There are two main ways of constructing a waterfall using pre-formed units: either

The material used to make a waterfall is best completely concealed. Here slabs of stone, pieces of natural rock and cobbles have been combined to good effect.

MOVING-WATER PROJECTS

Pond Filters and Water Clarifiers

If you plan to keep fish, particularly koi carp, a filter will be a great asset in removing their waste products from the pond. Indeed, where there are few or no pond plants and a high density of fish, a filter is essential. Filters can also be the solution to persistent green algae. Two types of filter are available: mechanical and biological. Both need to be operated in conjunction with a pump.

Mechanical Filters

Mechanical filters are cheaper and simpler than the biological type. Pumps are generally supplied complete with a small foam filter. Larger and more efficient foam filters can also be fitted to the water inlet of a submersible pump.

A larger filter typically consists of two deep plastic trays, one inside the other, filled with fine gravel or filter granules, and a layer of foam. This unit is placed in the pond and connected to the water inlet of the pump. Water is drawn through the filter material, which 'sieves out' waste particles and algae. The filter will need regular cleaning to remove accumulated debris, the regularity of which depends on the condition of the pond. Mechanical filters can be run intermittently and start becoming effective immediately the pump is switched on.

Biological Filters

Biological filters are dearer and more complex in their method of operation, but are more effective. Each consists of a large, lidded, plastic box which is housed outside the pond. The box contains layers of foam of varying density, or foam plus filter granules. Here colonies of natural bacteria break down the harmful waste products of fish and convert them to nitrates, which are then taken up by pond plants. Green algae and other waste particles are also removed.

There are two main drawbacks to this type of filter. First the pump must be run

by purchasing a complete waterfall unit, or by purchasing a small header pool and several bowls to form the cascade. The obvious drawback of a complete unit is that you're restricted to the designs available. If you're considering pre-formed units, it's worth reading the information on pre-formed pond materials on page 18, as waterfall units are constructed using the same materials. Bear in mind that the cheaper units have a limited life of several years, principally because cheaper plastics have less resistance to ultra-violet light, and in this situation much of the unit will be exposed to sunlight.

Flexible Liners

Flexible liners look most natural and attractive but do take more work to install, as it's necessary to design and shape the waterfall channel which is then made waterproof using the liner. The sides of the channel can be concealed with stones and plants, or the liner can be completely concealed by ornamental stone, as with our featured waterfall.

Choosing a Pump

There are general details on choosing pumps on page 56, which it's advisable to read first.

70

continuously, as the bacteria need a constant supply of oxygen and waste particles for food in order to survive. Second, biological filters are also bulky and can be hard to conceal, though manufacturers are devising ingenious solutions to the problem, such as concealing a filter within a pre-formed waterfall unit. Biological filters take several weeks to become effective as the colonies of bacteria take time to become established.

In a large specialist koi pond where no plants can be kept, one problem that can occur is an excess of the nitrates produced by a filter system, as there are no pond plants to take up the nitrates. A solution is to run the water through an additional filter bed containing oxygenating plants, before the water returns to the pond.

Ultra-violet (UV) Clarifiers

A biological filter removes the vast majority of green algae, but sometimes the tiniest species can still get through. If crystal-clear water is essential, a UV clarifier (sold by pond equipment suppliers) can be fitted in conjunction with an external filter. Clarifiers are also claimed to remove harmful bacteria.

Magnetic Water Treatments

Limescale deposits can be a nuisance with UV clarifiers and filter systems. A magnetic water treatment device is a relatively new introduction that fits between pump and filter, and reduces limescale build-up by affecting the structure of carbonates and bicarbonates that cause the scaling. One knock-on effect is that it reduces blanket weed, and indeed all plant growth, by changing the structure of nutrients. Another less welcome effect, however, is that carbonates and bicarbonates are part of the pond's pH buffering system, and their alteration can result in severe pH swings which are unhealthy for fish. More research is currently being done into the effects of magnetic water treatment.

To create a waterfall, the water is circulated by means of a submersible pump placed in the pond, which delivers water to the top of the fall via a concealed hose. From there the force of gravity carries the water down the cascade and into the pool. A submersible pump is adequate for most garden waterfalls, though a surface pump may be necessary for larger constructions.

The important factors when choosing a pump to power a waterfall are the height to which the pump can lift the water (the head) and the volume of water it can move (the flow rate, or amount of water flowing down the watercourse). The pump manufacturer's details usually quote a flow rate for the pump, and the head that the pump can produce at this flow rate. Choose a pump with a flow rate equal to or larger than your needs and check that the quoted head is at least a third larger than the height you need. The output of a larger pump can be throttled back by the control valve on the pump.

The flow rate of water required depends firstly on the width of the cascade – the wider the steps of the waterfall, the greater the volume needed to provide a continuous and effective flow. Obviously it's your choice whether to have a smaller and cheaper pump which will give a thin sheet of water, or a larger and more expensive

pump to provide a deep, flowing cascade. As a general guide, a pump that moves 1,350 litres (300 gallons) of water per hour will give a continuous sheet of water down a watercourse 30cm (1ft) wide if the watercourse surface is smooth, though approximately double this flow rate will be needed if the surface is uneven or rocky. It's obviously difficult to form a mental picture of volumes of water as they relate to your waterfall, but you can get some idea of flow rates by measuring the output of an ordinary garden hosepipe. Use a bucket or large watering can, and mark the 9-litre (2-gallon) level. Turn the hose on and time how long it takes to reach this level. If it takes 70 seconds, divide 3,600 (the number of seconds in an hour) by 70. Multiply the result by 9 (the number of litres) to give litres per hour. The result is 463 litres (102 gallons) per hour. Now, direct the hose down your waterfall. This will give a rough guide to the sort of flow rate you want.

Delivery Hose

There is a pressure loss across the hose and fittings which reduces the effective output head of the pump. This loss is greater with increased hose length and particularly with decreasing hose diameters. As a rough guide, choose a hose diameter equal to or larger than the diameter of the pump outlet for installations using short hose lengths. It may be

A waterfall need not be vast to be effective, even a couple of 'steps' will make a delightful feature.

> ## You Will Need
>
> *(Materials and instructions are for the construction of the waterfall only and do not include the pond itself)*
>
> *4 slabs of stone 45cm (18in) square and a maximum of 10cm (4in) thick. Weathered paving slabs could also be used*
>
> *4 pieces of flexible liner 90cm (3ft) square, for the steps of the watercourse (alternatively, use 1 large piece of liner if available)*
>
> *1 piece of flexible liner 1.2 × 1.5m (4 × 5ft), for the header pond*
>
> *Liner underlay, the same size as the liner*
>
> *Natural stone to edge the 'steps' of the waterfall*
>
> *1 submersible pump*
>
> *1 brick or block of wood*
>
> *Armoured electrical cable or cable plus conduit*
>
> *Waterproof/weatherproof connector*
>
> *Either a residual current detector if using a mains-voltage pump or a transformer if using a low-voltage pump*
>
> *Sufficient hose to run from the pump to the header pool*
>
> *Cobbles to line the pond edge (optional)*

necessary, depending on pump specification, to use larger-diameter hose where a longer delivery hose is required. In all cases the hose length should be no longer than necessary.

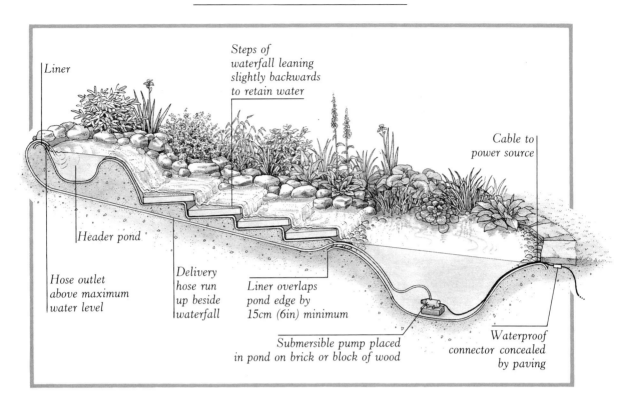

Liner

Steps of
waterfall leaning
slightly backwards
to retain water

Cable to
power source

Header pond

Hose outlet
above maximum
water level

Delivery
hose run
up beside
waterfall

Liner overlaps
pond edge by
15cm (6in) minimum

Submersible pump placed
in pond on brick or block of wood

Waterproof
connector concealed
by paving

IMPORTANT: Read the safety notes on page 55 before buying and installing the pump and fittings.

Step-by-step Construction

1 Excavate the steps of the watercourse. These should be 45cm (18in) square with 'steps' that are 15cm (6in) high, and constructed so the slabs will be slightly lower at the back than at the front lip. This ensures that some water will remain in the watercourse when the pump is switched off. Slope the sides of the channel at a gentle angle.

2 Excavate the small header pond at the top of the waterfall. It should be 60cm (2ft) wide, 90cm (3ft) long and 30cm (1ft) deep.

3 Make sure that the 'steps' and header pond are correctly shaped, remove any sharp stones or other objects that could puncture the liner. Line the watercourse with underlay, then fit the flexible liner, starting with the lowest piece. This should overlap the edge of the pool, and the higher pieces should overlap the lower ones. Allow a liner overlap of 15cm (6in) so that the construction is watertight.

At the edges of the 'steps' bury the edges of the liner in the soil so that it is secured and concealed. Make sure that the rim of the liner will be above the maximum water level.

4 Install the electrical supply to the pump, following steps 1–4 on page 59.

5 Place the pump in the pond on a brick or block of wood so that the water inlet is above the debris that naturally accumulates on the floor of the pond. The pump should be as near as possible to the base of the waterfall so that the delivery hose is no longer than is necessary.

6 Connect the hose to the pump's outlet, and run the hose out of the pond and up beside the waterfall into the header pond. Take care not to squeeze or kink the hose as it will restrict the flow of water. The end of the hose should be above the maximum water level of the header pond, or water will be siphoned back down to the pond when the pump is switched off.

7 Position the rocks to conceal the edges of the steps and the hose, and to prevent soil falling into the water. Take care that there are no sharp edges that could damage the liner.

PLANTING

An artificially created mound of soil tends to be reasonably dry in the vast majority of cases, so avoid using moisture-loving plants in such a situation. Instead use a selection of the smaller plants described in the section on plants to associate with ponds. Plant compact shrubs with attractive foliage such as Acer palmatum 'Dissectum' varieties (Japanese maples) – the two in our picture have lovely purple foliage. Dwarf bamboos would contrast well, as would several of the golden-foliaged grasses such as Hakonochloa. Add a touch of brighter colour with herbaceous perennials such as dicentras, with their colourful locket-shaped flowers.

Trailing, ground-hugging plants look good on rockeries in particular. Lysimachia nummularia (creeping jenny) is a vigorous spreading plant that forms a carpet of bright green foliage studded with golden flowers in summer. Ajuga varieties (bugle) mostly have purple, dark green or variegated foliage, and make a good foil to other plants as well as looking good in their own right. Vinca minor (lesser periwinkle) forms an evergreen carpet of glossy green foliage that is covered with blue flowers in spring – there are varieties with variegated foliage, white or purple flowers too.

PROJECT NINE

A Cobblestone Fountain

A cobblestone fountain is a versatile little feature which can be incorporated in a variety of surroundings. Its size can be varied to suit the space available, down to as little as 45cm (18in) across.

A water feature of this type has several advantages over a pond. The reservoir of water is securely covered and therefore safe where there are young children, the construction is simple and economic, and very little maintenance is required. On the debit side, aquatic plants cannot be grown as there is no accessible water, but you can more than compensate for this by surrounding such a feature with plants that possess bold, handsome foliage in cool colours for maximum effect.

The construction of a cobblestone feature is quite straightforward. Water is contained in a reservoir directly below ground, and because it is out of sight the material used is unimportant so long as it is watertight. A plastic dustbin, wooden half-barrel, central heating tank or similar container is perfectly adequate, or a flexible liner could be used instead. The water is moved by a submersible pump placed in the reservoir, with the fountain jet protruding just above ground level. A piece of steel mesh covers the water completely, then cobbles are placed on top so that the mesh cannot be seen. Powered by the pump, water gushes up through the stones, splashes over them and back into the reservoir. A more dramatic effect can be achieved by fitting the pump outlet with a geyser jet, so that the water gushes up in a most impressive fashion. Access to electricity is obviously essential to power the pump. It's also useful to have a nearby source of water as its constant circulation over stones results in a steady loss by evaporation, so the reservoir will need regular topping up.

Opposite: Cobblestone features are not only quick and relatively inexpensive, but are also safe for young children.

Left: A millstone feature is constructed in a similar way to a cobblestone feature and makes an excellent centrepiece for a garden.

A Millstone Feature

A similar but more elaborate feature can be constructed using a millstone for the centrepiece, surrounded by a bed of cobbles. Construction is along the same lines, though with additional supports for the millstone, and the pump is fitted with an outlet hose that directs water through the stone's central hole. A millstone looks extremely handsome but can be costly, though it's worth shopping around as prices vary substantially. Imitation millstones made of fibreglass and coated with sand are available, but obviously don't look as good as the real thing – make sure that you see a fake millstone in the flesh before purchasing it.

Choosing a Pump

There are general details on choosing a pump on page 56, which it's advisable to read first.

A small and relatively inexpensive pump is required for a feature of this size. Do think carefully, however, about the effect you wish to create – whether you opt for one of the smallest pumps that will give a small bubbling jet of water, or choose a reasonably powerful pump to give a more dramatic, foaming fountain. Choice of fountain jet may also affect your choice of pump: make sure that your desired jet and pump are compatible, as certain jets need a more powerful pump.

IMPORTANT: Read the safety notes on page 55 before buying and installing a pump and fittings.

You Will Need

1 submersible pump

1 jet attachment for the pump (optional)

Either a residual current detector if using a mains-voltage pump or a transformer if using a low-voltage pump

Sufficient armoured cable or cable plus conduit to reach your power source

Waterproof/weatherproof connector

Spirit level

Water reservoir – use whatever is cheapest and easiest to obtain, so long as it is durable and waterproof, such as a plastic dustbin. If using flexible liner, calculate the amount of liner and underlay required using the formula on page 27.

1 brick or block of wood

Piece of heavy-gauge steel mesh, large enough to overlap the reservoir by at least 15cm (6in) on all sides, and more in the case of large features

Sufficient cobbles to cover the entire feature. These can be purchased from a variety of sources, including garden centres. Do not remove cobbles from sea defences

Step-by-step Construction

1 Measure the dimensions of the container that is to be your water reservoir and excavate a hole to match. Firm the floor of the excavation well to ensure that there is no danger of subsidence.

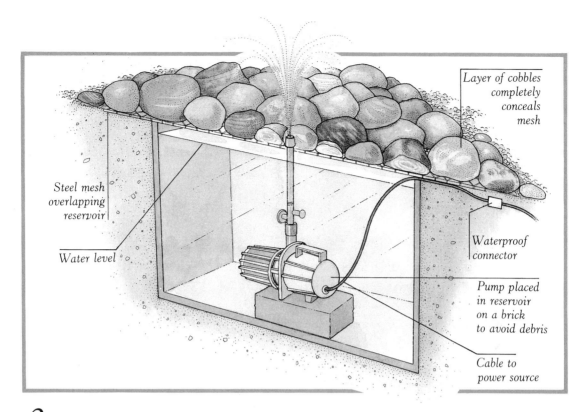

Layer of cobbles
completely
conceals
mesh

Steel mesh
overlapping
reservoir

Water level

Waterproof
connector

Pump placed
in reservoir
on a brick
to avoid debris

Cable to
power source

2 Sink the container so that the rim is at ground level, and use the spirit level to check that it is level. Fill the reservoir with water.

3 Install the electrical supply and pump, following steps 1–4 on page 59.

4 Place the pump in the reservoir on a brick or block of wood to keep the water inlet above any debris that may accumulate. The fountain head should be central and just above ground level.

5 Place the steel mesh over the reservoir, leaving an overlap of at least 15cm (6in) on all sides to give the mesh sufficient support. Cover the entire mesh area with cobbles, leaving a small space for the fountain head.

PLANTING

A cobblestone feature is set off to perfection by a selection of plants with attractive foliage and shapes, such as ornamental grasses and herbaceous perennials like hostas, which are mentioned in the section on plants to associate with ponds (page 112). All the smaller plants listed there would also be suitable for growing in containers if there were no soil surrounding the feature.

A Wall Fountain

 A wall fountain is a supremely elegant feature that fits easily into a small space. It is ideal for a courtyard or town garden.

Our wall feature is ornamental and fairly elaborate. The water is moved by a submersible pump in the pool and delivered to the mask via a hose which is concealed by the trellis arch. The water trickles through the carved mask of an animal's head into the scallop shell fixed to the wall below, and finally splashes into a raised pond. A small trellis arch wreathed in climbers makes an ideal frame for the ornaments and adds the finishing touch to the whole feature. The whitewashed walls give this sunny courtyard corner a real lift, setting off the planting to perfection and imbuing it with an exotic Mediterranean feel. The water reservoir is a raised pond built of bricks that have been whitewashed to blend in with the surrounding walls. If you don't fancy bricklaying, it is possible to buy a ready-made semi-circular pond made of concrete.

Choosing a Pump

There are general details on choosing a pump on page 56, which it's advisable to read first.

This wall fountain is quite elaborate, but a similar feature can be constructed on a smaller scale if desired.

The important point to bear in mind when selecting a pump for a wall fountain is that the pump should be sufficiently powerful to lift the water to the height of the mask. Therefore choose a pump with a head height at least a third higher than the mask to allow enough leeway. Remember that a pump can always be throttled back but cannot be powered up. The flow rate is less important as only a small volume of water needs to be moved.

IMPORTANT: **Read the safety notes on page 55 before buying and installing the pump and fittings.**

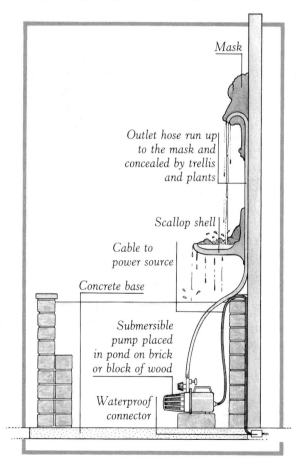

Mask

Outlet hose run up to the mask and concealed by trellis and plants

Scallop shell

Cable to power source

Concrete base

Submersible pump placed in pond on brick or block of wood

Waterproof connector

You Will Need

(Materials and construction details cover the fountain and its surround only, and do not include the pond or reservoir of water)

1 piece of decorative trellis arch

Wooden battens or 'spacers' for the trellis, 1cm (½in) thick

Screws and wall plugs to attach the trellis, mask and shell to the wall

1 mask or gargoyle. There is a variety of styles available, made of terracotta, lead, stone, reconstituted stone or plastic. A mask should have a spout, and a channel at the back to house the delivery hose

1 scallop shell of the same material (optional)

1 submersible pump

Sufficient electric cable to reach your power source

Armoured cable or waterproof cable plus conduit

Waterproof/weatherproof connector

Either a residual current detector if using a mains-voltage pump or a transformer if using a low-voltage pump

1.8m (6ft) of hose, the size of which must be compatible with the pump outlet

1 brick or block of wood

Step-by-step Construction

1 Check that the pointing and brickwork of the wall are sound. If fixing a wall fountain to a house wall in particular, it may be advisable to treat the wall with a waterproofing solution to avoid potential damp problems.

2 Fix the trellis to the wall using screws and wall plugs. Use 1-cm- (½-in-) thick wooden battens between the trellis and wall to allow space for the climbing plants to twine.

3 Attach the hose to the spout of the mask, and fix the mask and shell to the wall. Ensure that the ornaments are fixed so that water does not splash directly on to the wall.

4 Tuck the hose just under the trellis and run it down into the pond. There are several other ways of concealing the hose. If you have a cavity wall made of two parallel courses of brick, drill a hole behind the mask, another hole directly below and just above the level of the water, and pull the hose through the wall cavity by means of a piece of string. If you have access to the back of the wall, drill right though it to run the hose up out of sight.

5 Install the electrical supply and pump, following steps 1–4 on page 59.

6 Place the pump in the pond or reservoir on a brick or block of wood. Attach

---

PLANTING

The planting for a feature of this type is an essential ingredient in its success – imagine it with no plants at all, and the effect would be stark and rather unappealing. The climbing plants for the trellis shouldn't be too vigorous, as this is a decorative part of the feature that should be emphasized rather than smothered. A clematis is ideal: the ruby-red flowers in the photograph belong to Clematis 'Niobe'. This could be planted with a variegated ivy such as Hedera helix 'Goldheart'.

Aquatic plants should also be chosen carefully. Tall, grassy-leaved plants frame the trellis and ornaments. Choose an elegant grass such as Scirpus 'Zebrinus', with Butomus umbellatus (flowering rush). One or two bushy marginal plants soften the outside edge of the pond; in the picture is Primula florindae (giant Himalayan cowslip) bearing nodding yellow heads of delicately fragrant flowers. Other good plants to choose include Caltha palustris (kingcup) which has golden flowers, Houttuynia 'Chameleon' with its red and green leaves, or Preslia cervina with its blue flowers and minty aromatic foliage. A compact water lily can be placed in the deepest part of the pond, such as Nymphaea 'Solfatare', which bears yellow pink-flushed blooms.

Planting

THE ATTRACTION OF a pond can be far more than the water alone. Once you have a pond, you can grow a wonderful selection of aquatic and moisture-loving plants with colourful flowers and foliage, that combine to make your pond into a truly stunning feature. Not only are aquatic plants immensely ornamental, but they are also essential to create a balance of nature in your pond, ensuring that it stays healthy with the minimum of maintenance. Aquatic plants are broadly divided into four groups as follows:

Deep-water aquatics, which need to be placed with their crowns at least 30cm (1ft) below the surface of the water. Most of this group consists of the many different water lilies (*Nymphaea*).

Oxygenating plants, which also grow in water at least 30cm (1ft) deep. These are mostly functional rather than ornamental, as they are particularly good at removing mineral salts and waste products from the water.

Marginal plants, which grow in shallow water, usually around the pond's edges.

A pond can add a new dimension to the planting in your garden, particularly with a bog garden which enables you to grow many stunning, moisture-loving plants with bold, handsome foliage.

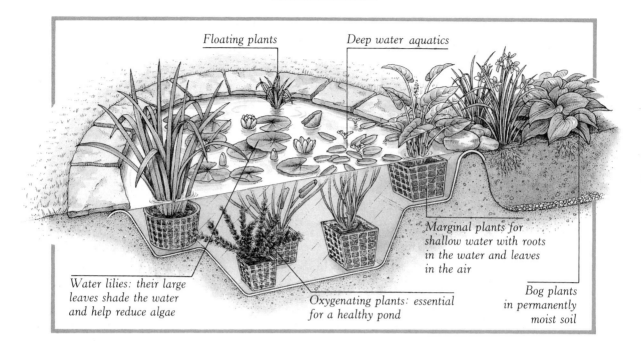

Floating plants

Deep water aquatics

Water lilies: their large leaves shade the water and help reduce algae

Oxygenating plants: essential for a healthy pond

Marginal plants for shallow water with roots in the water and leaves in the air

Bog plants in permanently moist soil

They need to have their roots in the water, and their leaves in the air.

Floating plants, which are free-floating and do not need planting.

All these plants actually grow in the water itself. An additional group usually cultivated in conjunction with ponds is bog plants (also called marsh or poolside plants), which need permanently moist soil. Many bog plants have colourful flowers and lush attractive foliage, and they make the perfect transition between pond and garden if the soil is naturally moist, or in a specially created bog garden. Some marginal plants also grow happily in very boggy soil.

All these groups of plants are covered in detail in the following pages. The plants have been chosen very much with the ornamental garden pond in mind, so

varieties that are very invasive or of lesser ornamental value have not been included. Because the planting adjacent to the pond itself makes an important contribution to the whole effect, there is also a special section describing other garden plants that associate particularly well with water (see page 112).

Using Plants to Create a Healthy Pond

Plants are vital in order to have a naturally healthy, balanced pond, and to provide a habitable environment for fish and wildlife. Without any plants at all the whole surface area of the pond is open to sunlight which encourages the rapid proliferation of green algae. These algae thrive on mineral salts that occur naturally in water – particularly in fresh tap water – and can quickly turn the pond into a green soup. Algae are not actually harmful to the pond's inhabitants unless the infestation is severe, but they do make it hard to see anything in the water and detract from the pond's overall appearance.

Ideally around a third to a half of the pond's surface should be covered with aquatic plant foliage to prevent sunlight reaching too much of the water. The large rounded leaves of water lilies are particularly useful for providing fast cover. Oxygenating plants are excellent at combating the growth of algae and maintaining a healthy pond, a function they perform by removing mineral salts from the water – they have larger appetites than algae for these mineral salts and eventually starve them out.

BUYING AND PLANTING AQUATIC PLANTS

Spring to early summer is the best time to plant up a pond. The water is sufficiently warm to provide a receptive environment for new plants, which then have the whole summer and autumn to establish themselves before winter comes. If your pond has just been filled with water, allow it to stand for a few days so that the temperature of the water stabilizes.

Buying Tips

When you purchase aquatic plants, there are a few useful tips that are well worth bearing in mind. Some may seem a little obvious, but a number of garden centres and nurseries unfortunately don't look after their aquatic plants as well as they should.

First take a quick look around the display of aquatic plants. Marginal and deep-water aquatics are usually displayed in trays of water, which should be reasonably clean. Don't buy plants if the trays contain lots of dead rotting vegetation and green weed or algae, which is a sure sign of neglect. The soil of aquatic plants should be permanently moist, so avoid like the plague any which have been allowed to dry out.

Plants should look fresh and healthy with plenty of new growth: avoid any with a lot of dead leaves that could have already spread disease through the entire plant. Plants should be clearly labelled, but don't buy any with badly faded labels – a clear indicator that they've been sitting around for a long time. Finally do make sure that your plants aren't bringing unwanted guests to your pond. Duckweed is the main offender that can be carried on other plants – a minuscule, bright green floating plant that tends to sneak in quietly but can soon carpet the entire surface of a pond. If you're not happy with your local source of supply of aquatic plants, it's well worth considering a trip to a water plant specialist or ordering plants by mail order (see the list of suppliers on page 125).

Plant up your aquatic plants immediately after purchasing. If you cannot do this for a day or two, place them in a bucket of water. Don't leave them in plastic bags or allow them to dry out.

Planning Your Planting

It's easy to think of pond plants as a totally separate entity from the rest of your garden, but do bear in mind that your pond and its planting will be seen in the context of their surroundings. Beware of creating colour clashes: a red water lily with the bright mauve flowers of *Lythrum salicaria* (purple loosestrife), for example, would look hideous.

To get the best out of your pond planting, consider how plants can be grouped together to look most attractive. As well as getting the flower colours to blend and contrast well, don't forget the actual shapes of the plants. By grouping plants of contrasting shape – spiky-leaved iris with the rounded form of houttuynias and prostrate myosotis, for example – you will achieve an attractive effect whether or not there is anything in flower. Foliage colour as well as shape should be borne in mind too: it's easy to be dazzled by magnificent flowers, but colourful foliage will look good for months rather than weeks. There are lots of tips on plant associations throughout the sections on different types of plants.

How to Plant

Aquatic plants for ornamental garden ponds are best planted in special mesh containers, which come in a wide range of shapes and sizes. Some retailers now sell plants already in mesh pots, which can be placed directly in the pond. Planted containers can be positioned in the pond at the desired point, and can easily be moved when any cleaning or maintenance is necessary. A particular advantage of planting individual plants in containers is that each one is shown off at its best. Don't plant two or more different varieties in the same basket – plants grow at different rates, so one is almost bound to smother the others. Always use special mesh baskets for aquatics. Don't use solid plant pots as aquatics need to have free passage of their roots through the sides as well as the bottom of the pot.

There are two alternatives to planting in containers, though both have drawbacks. The first is to put a layer of soil about 15cm (6in) deep on the base of the pond, planting directly into the soil and filling the pond very slowly over a couple of weeks. The main problem here is that eventually the plants will grow into each other, with more vigorous varieties smothering their companions. The only solution is to control plants on a regular basis, and weeding a murky pond over your elbows in water is not an appealing task! This method is really suitable only for a wildlife pond, where the planting is, for the most part, left to its own devices.

The second option for marginal and bog plants is to construct integral planting pockets around the pond edges when installing the pond, or to buy a pre-formed pond with a 'marsh pocket' built in around the edge. Here similar problems of tangling and overgrowth can occur, though

The contrast between foliage shapes and colours is as important as flower colour. Hostas, iris and water lilies are central to this attractive planting.

plants are more accessible and therefore more easily controlled. A good compromise is to sink plants in mesh containers into these marsh pockets, concealing the containers with soil and gravel.

PLANTING DEEP WATER AND MARGINAL AQUATICS

You Will Need

1 mesh container for each plant. Mesh containers are available in many different shapes and sizes to fit your pond. Older-style containers are made of wider mesh and will need lining first. Newer models made of fine mesh are now available which don't need to be lined

Hessian or fine plastic mesh for lining if necessary

Soil for planting. You can purchase bags of aquatic planting compost, which is ideal. Good garden loam can be used – it should be roughly sifted to remove any debris such as roots, leaves and stones. Don't use sandy or clay soil. Avoid ordinary potting compost, and garden soil which has been manured or fertilized over the past year or your pond will receive a large dose of algae-boosting nutrients. Lastly avoid soil which has recently been treated with chemicals

Fine (pea) gravel to cover the surface of the planted container

Step-by-step Planting

1 Line the containers if necessary.

2 Prepare the plants by trimming off dead or damaged foliage. With water lilies, remove all the large adult leaves. Remove solid pots before planting, taking care to disturb the roots as little as possible. Mesh pots can be left on, as the roots will simply grow through into the new soil.

3 When planting tall marginals, place stones in the base of the container for added stability.

4 Put a layer of soil in the base of the container, then place the plant in the container, ensuring that its existing soil level is just below the rim. Fill with soil to within 2.5cm (1in) of the top of the container and gently firm the soil.

5 Add fine gravel to just below the rim of the pot. This stops soil floating out of the pot, prevents fish nosing around and stirring up the soil, and provides an attractive finish.

6 Water the plants thoroughly with a fine spray, to soak the compost and drive out surplus air.

7 Place the plants in the pond. Marginal and oxygenating plants can be placed directly in their final position. Deep-water aquatics need to be acclimatized gradually to their eventual planting position: do this by placing the planted containers on several bricks, so that the plants' foliage is just below the surface. Remove the bricks one by one over the course of several weeks as the leaves reach the surface. Remember to place some padding under the bricks so that the pond doesn't become damaged.

For larger ponds where this method isn't practical, suspend plants in the water by running a line of stout string on either side of the basket and anchoring it on opposite sides of the pond (this is best done by two people). Lower the plant gradually as the leaves extend until it reaches its final position, when the string can be removed.

Planting Bunched Oxygenators

Most oxygenating plants are sold as bunches of unrooted cuttings with a weight at one end. To plant these, prepare a container as described above and loosely fill with soil. Insert about 7.5cm (3in) of the weighted end of the cuttings into the soil, firm gently and proceed as from step 4 above. Oxygenating plants can be planted directly in their final position in water that is 30–60cm (1–2ft) deep.

WATER LILIES

Some of the most attractive pond plants can be grown in the deepest part of the pond. Everyone's favourite is the water lily (*Nymphaea*). This is the true aristocrat of the pond, bearing exotic perfectly-shaped flowers that are a mass of silky petals around a central group of colourful stamens. These stunning blooms are produced from early to late summer and float on the water's surface surrounded by rafts of rounded leaves or 'lily pads'. As well as being seductively beautiful, water lilies have a very practical role to play in maintaining the pond's health. Their large leaves are especially useful for screening the water from sunlight and thereby hindering the growth of green algae. Fish benefit from the shade and can also shelter from predators. Frogs, toads and even small birds use the leaves as natural rafts.

Water lilies need a sunny site in order to flower well, and they also dislike a lot of moving churning water. They are therefore best sited away from waterfalls and fountains. Water lilies are fairly costly; the most vigorous varieties are cheaper but these are suitable only for the largest garden ponds – don't be tempted to buy one of these larger cheaper varieties unless you have a pond to match.

There is a vast range of different varieties and sizes, so take care to choose the right size for your pond. A selection of the best available varieties is described here, and for ease of choice it's broadly divided into four groups according to the size of pond that suits them best. Water lilies, however, are variable and cannot easily be pigeonholed, so treat these sizes as a general guide only.

Small water lilies are suitable for miniature ponds such as barrels, tubs and sinks. The smallest varieties should be planted in 15cm (6in) of water; others prefer to be planted in 23–30cm (9–12in) of water. They have a spread of around 30–60cm (1–2ft). This shallow depth of planting means that in tiny pools the lilies may be frozen and killed in winter, so it's best to protect them in some way. Either drain the mini-pool in autumn

Left: N. *'James Brydon'* is one of the best water lilies for small to medium ponds.

Opposite: Nymphaea pygmaea *'Helvola'* is a true miniature that thrives in the tiniest of ponds.

Below: N. *'Froebeli'* is a superb variety which is exceptionally free-flowering and ideal for small ponds.

and cover the lily with a thick mat of straw, or lift the plant and keep it in water in a cool frost-free place.

Compact water lilies are ideal for small garden ponds, and should be planted in water 30–45cm (12–18in) deep. They have a spread of 60–90cm (2–3ft). If there is any danger of the plant becoming frozen in winter, protect as above.

Medium water lilies are suitable for ponds with an approximate size of 1.8 × 2.4m (6 × 8ft). They should be planted in 45–75cm (18–30in) depth of water, and have a spread of 90–120cm (3–4ft).

Vigorous water lilies are suitable only for the largest ponds with a minimum area of 3 square m (32 square ft), and should be planted in water that is at least 60cm (2ft) deep. They have a spread of 1.2–1.8m (4–6ft) and often more when well established.

IMPORTANT: See step 7 about planting deep-water aquatics on page 90.

Small Water Lilies

Nymphaea Candida is a dainty variety that bears small, pure white, cup-shaped flowers with contrasting red stigmas.

N. 'Laydekeri' varieties are excellent for tiny ponds as they are very free-flowering with comparatively little foliage, and they are also happy in slightly larger ponds. Two of the best are N. 'Laydekeri Purpurata', which produces rosy-crimson flowers that are slightly flecked with white, and N. 'Laydekeri Rosea', which bears scented soft rose-pink flowers. The flowers of N. 'Laydekeri Lilacea' are deeper pink and are also scented. N. 'Laydekeri Fulgens' has bright magenta-crimson flowers with orange-red stamens.

N. *pygmaea* 'Helvola' is a true miniature that is particularly attractive; it bears soft yellow flowers of a similar size and dark green leaves with maroon splashes. Two other varieties are slightly larger: *N.p.* 'Alba' bears delicate, star-like, white, gold-centred flowers that are the size of a medallion, and light green foliage; the flowers of *N.p.* 'Rubra' open rose-pink in the centre and the paler outer petals turn rich red as they age. These varieties need a minimum water depth of 15cm (6in).

Compact Water Lilies

N. 'Aurora' is an excellent variety that bears changeable flowers. On the first day they open yellow, turning to orange the next day, and finally becoming dark blood-red on the third day. The dark green leaves are attractively mottled with purple.

N. 'Froebeli' bears striking deep blood-red flowers against dark reddish-green leaves. This is an especially good, fragrant, free-flowering variety which deserves to be grown much more widely.

N. 'Graziella' has cup-shaped reddish-orange flowers that pale with age, and also produces olive-green leaves heavily splashed with purple.

N. 'Hermine' bears pure white star-shaped flowers and dark green oval leaves. It also tolerates partial shade.

N. 'James Brydon' is one of the most popular of all water lilies, partly because of its ability to grow in partial shade as well as in sun. It produces handsome carmine-red flowers and purplish leaves.

N. odorata 'Firecrest' produces unusually coloured flowers, red streaked with pink and with prominent red-tipped stamens. These distinctive blooms have the bonus of being fragrant. N.o. var. rosea bears deep rose-pink flowers against purple-green foliage.

N. 'Rose Arey' bears large, deep rose-pink flowers with orange stamens, which are strongly scented. This is an excellent variety and one of the best pinks.

N. 'Sioux' has changeable flowers that first open soft yellow flushed with red, then develop to an attractive coppery-red.

N. 'Solfatare' has pale yellow flowers flushed with pink, and bears leaves heavily splashed with purple-red blotches.

Medium Water Lilies

N. 'Conqueror' has bright red flowers flecked with white. This variety is especially free-flowering.

N. 'Gonnêre' (also called 'Snowball') is one of the best whites, bearing magnificent double pure white flowers.

N. 'Marliacea Albida' bears many large, gleaming white flowers which have a delicate fragrance. N. 'Marliacea Chromatella' has soft primrose-yellow flowers with brighter yellow stamens. The leaves are splashed with bronze markings. N. 'Marliacea Rosea' bears fragrant, rich rose-pink flowers.

N. odorata 'William B. Shaw' bears pale shell-pink, fragrant flowers that deepen in colour towards the centre.

N. 'Paul Hariot' is an excellent changeable variety. The flowers open buff-yellow, changing to orange-pink the next day, and eventually darken to pinkish-red on following days. The leaves are spotted with reddish-purple.

N. 'Rose Nymphe' bears deep rose-pink flowers that are also fragrant.

Vigorous Water Lilies

N. alba, the native European water lily, bears white flowers up to 15cm (6in) across, with yellow stamens. It is a strong-growing variety that can be acclimatized to grow in up to 1.8m (6ft) of water.

N. 'Attraction' is a very handsome variety that has glowing deep red flowers up to 20cm (8in) across, with reddish stamens tipped with yellow. On young plants the flowers can be pink and smaller so don't think you've been given the wrong variety!

N. 'Charles de Meurville' is an extremely vigorous variety with wine-red flowers, streaked with white, up to 25cm (10in) across.

N. 'Colossea' bears fragrant blush-pink flowers that pale with age, freely borne from spring to autumn. This variety is very vigorous and only for the largest ponds; it can be acclimatized to grow in up to 1.8m (6ft) of water.

N. 'Escarboucle' is a handsome, very free-flowering variety that has huge, fragrant, deep crimson flowers up to 25cm (10in) across.

N. 'Gladstoniana' bears pure white flowers that can be up to 30cm (1ft) across, with masses of golden stamens. This variety is suitable only for very large ponds, and can be acclimatized to grow in up to 1.8m (6ft) of water.

N. 'Marliacea Carnea' (also known as 'Morning Glory') has lovely pale pink flowers that have a deeper pink tinge at the base of the petals.

OTHER DEEP-WATER AQUATICS

There are several other aquatic plants that need to be planted in at least 30cm (1ft) of water. They can be grown in addition to water lilies if space allows, and several are suitable for growing in sites that water lilies dislike, such as in partial shade or in moving water.

Aponogeton distachyos (water hawthorn) is a delightful plant worth growing just for the rich vanilla scent of the flowers, which are white with black stamens. These are mostly produced through summer, but sometimes also appear in spring and even in winter. The strap-shaped green leaves and the flowers float on the water's surface. Planting depth 23–45cm (9–18in), spread 60cm (2ft).

Nuphar varieties (pond lilies) shouldn't be confused with water lilies, as their globe-shaped yellow flowers are 2.5–5cm (1–2in) across and nowhere near as showy. They are still attractive and useful plants, however, especially as they grow in shade and moving water. The flowers are produced in summer. N. pumila is suitable for most garden ponds. Planting depth 45–60cm (1½–2ft), spread 60cm (2ft). N. lutea (brandy bottle) is much more vigorous and should be grown only in a very large pond or small lake. Planting depth up to 1.2m (4ft).

Nymphoides peltata (water fringe or floating heart). This fast-growing plant has leaves about 5cm (2in) across that resemble those of a water lily and in late summer bears many yellow flowers rather like those of a very handsome buttercup. It is an excellent plant for giving fast surface cover, hence it is useful in new pools. It is, however, very invasive and almost impossible to eradicate, so plant it only in a container and, if you can, prune it regularly in later years. Planting depth 45–60cm (1½–2ft).

Orontium aquaticum (golden club) is a most attractive plant that produces unusual flowers, rather like yellow-topped white pokers, that are borne in late spring. These stand 30cm (1ft) above the handsome, waxy green leaves that float on the surface. Planting depth 30–45cm

Left: Aponogeton (water hawthorn) is a deep-water plant with beautiful white, scented flowers in summer and autumn.

Opposite: This sumptuous blue-flowered iris looks perfect with the yellow-flowered mimulus.

(1–1½ft). It will also grow at the water's edge in shallow water, where it will hold its flowers and foliage well above the water.

MARGINAL PLANTS

Marginal aquatic plants are so called because they need to grow in shallow water at the pond's edge, with their feet in the water and their heads in the air. It's worth having a pond just to be able to grow some of these beautiful plants, and they have the added bonus of staying fresh-looking through even the driest of summers. There is an excellent range available with something for all tastes and situations, from bold striking foliage plants ideal for formal ponds to exuberant growers that blend well with the controlled tangle of an informal garden.

Marginal plants soften and conceal the sometimes harsh edges of a pond, and they also offer valuable shelter to all sorts of wildlife. Plants that produce straight vertical leaves provide a breeding ground for dragonflies, those dazzling aerial acrobats, and the smaller electric blue damselflies. These insects amply repay your hospitality by eating midges and mosquitos.

Most marginals prefer a sunny site. Some will grow in partial shade, and this is mentioned where relevant in the individual plant details. Sizes given are approximate, and the spread refers to the size the plant will attain if *not* restricted by a container. For details of how to plant marginals see page 90.

Calla palustris (bog arum) is particularly good at concealing pond edges with its thick scrambling stems. These are clothed with heart-shaped, glossy, dark green leaves, which provide a good backcloth for the small white spathes of flowers that are borne in late summer, similar to those of an arum lily. The flowers are followed by striking clusters of red berries. Height and spread 30cm (1ft).

Caltha palustris (marsh marigold, kingcup) is the earliest marginal plant to flower, bearing many clusters of bright sovereign-gold flowers in early spring against rounded, glossy, green leaves. This plant is popular with bees seeking food early in the year. Height and spread 30–45cm (1–1½ft). *C.p.* 'Flore Plena' bears double yellow 'pompon' flowers. There is a single white form, *C.p.* 'Alba',

but this tends to be a bit of a 'poor doer'. These varieties can be grown in ponds of any size, in shallow water or boggy soil. They prefer sun but will grow in partial shade. They look wonderful planted next to *Myosotis* (water forget-me-not) which bears delicate blue flowers.

The monster of the *Caltha* family is *C. polypetala*, which produces leaves almost 30cm (1ft) across and large clusters of yellow flowers that appear later in spring than those of other varieties. This potentially invasive plant is definitely for those with a larger pond. Height and spread 90cm (3ft).

Houttuynia cordata is a useful spreading plant for shallow water or moist soil, but I definitely recommend growing it in a container because of its invasive tendencies. The small heart-shaped leaves give off a

pungent orange smell when crushed. *H.c.* 'Flore Pleno' has bluish-green leaves, and produces small, white, cone-shaped flowers, as does *H.c.* 'Chameleon' (also called 'Harlequin' or 'Variegata'). This is the most striking variety, with dark green leaves brightly coloured with red and creamy-yellow. The red tints are less pronounced if this plant is grown with its roots in soil rather than in water. The colouring contrasts beautifully with golden-foliaged grasses in a bog garden. Houttuynias prefer partial shade. Height 15–30cm (6–12in), spread indefinite.

Irises are glorious plants with stunning flowers and bold foliage – there's little to beat them for summer colour. There are a number of attractive varieties from which to choose, and it's worth including one at least in your pond planting.

Iris laevigata bears large flowers 5–10cm (2–4in) across, which are rich blue with golden markings. *I.l.* 'Variegata' also has blue flowers, plus green-and-white-striped leaves. *I.l.* 'Snowdrift' produces pure white flowers, and those of *I.l.* 'Rose Queen' are deep old-rose pink.

I. ensata (also called *I. kaempferi*) bears flowers which are especially handsome, dark purple-blue richly marked with a variety of colours – white, yellow, red and blue – that can look like giant exotic butterflies. *I.e.* 'Variegata' produces rich purple flowers that show off well against its green-and-white-striped foliage. A number of fabulous named varieties such as *I.e.* 'Higo' bear sumptuous flowers up to 25cm (10in) across; unfortunately such large flowers can often become battered by rain and wind, and rarely have the chance to give of their best in a garden situation. Although this species is happy in water during the summer months, the rootball is best kept just moist during winter. It also needs lime-free soil.

I. versicolor bears neatly formed flowers with blue and purple petals splashed with yellow at the base. Those of *I.v.* 'Kermesina' are a showy deep plum-purple.

I. pseudacorus (yellow flag iris) is a large and vigorous plant with bright yellow flowers which isn't really ornamental enough for a garden pond. More worthwhile is the unattractively named *I.p.* var. *bastardii*, which bears creamy-yellow flowers. Where space is limited choose *I.p.* 'Variegata', which possesses handsome green-and-yellow-striped leaves. The variegation fades later in the summer.

Height of all varieties 60–90cm (2–3ft), spread approximately 60cm (2ft).

Lysichitum americanus goes by the unappealing common name of 'skunk cabbage', so be warned! In early spring it makes a superb show when its large, bright yellow spathes of arum lily-like flowers appear almost magically from bare ground, but they do give off an unpleasant scent – hence this plant's common name. Large, fresh green leaves up to 1.2m (4ft) high are produced after the flowers.

L. camtschatcensis bears spathes of white flowers that fortunately have a more pleasant scent, but they don't look as striking as those of the yellow-flowered species. This variety is often happier grown in marshy soil at the pond's edge. Lysichitums prefer sun but tolerate semi-shade. Height and spread up to 1.2m (4ft).

Lythrum salicaria (purple loosestrife) is a lovely, informal plant that is perfect for a cottage-style planting or a wildlife pond, especially as the tall spires of reddish-pink flowers produced in mid- to late summer are attractive to bees. This plant is happy in shallow water or boggy soil, in sun or part-shade. It can self-seed readily, so cut off dead flower heads before seeding. There are several named varieties such as *L.* 'The Rocket' and *L.* 'Firecandle' that have a more compact habit. Height 90cm (3ft), spread 45cm (1½ft)

Mentha aquatica (water mint) produces lavender-pink flowers, like tiny powder puffs, which are borne in summer and are also attractive to bees. The rounded, green, purple-tinged leaves give off a deliciously pungent scent when crushed. Like most of the mint family, this vigorous species is keen to spread, so grow it in a container and trim off any long rambling stems. It is another good plant for an informal planting, in sun or shade, and its scrambling stems go well with plants such as lysichitum and iris that have bold architectural leaves. Height 30–45cm (1–1½ft), spread indefinite.

Menyanthes trifoliata (bog bean or buck bean) is a useful scrambler for covering the pond edge with its creeping stems

clothed with glossy green leaves. Clusters of white, fringed flowers are borne on short spikes in spring. This plant makes a particularly good contrast to the vertical stems of grasses and irises. Height 23cm (9in), spread 30cm (1ft).

Myosotis scorpioides (also known as *M. palustris*, water forget-me-not) forms spreading carpets of flowers and foliage on the water's surface. In early to mid-summer it bears many little clusters of charming pale blue flowers, very similar to the popular garden forget-me-not. It also grows in very marshy soil. A newer variety, *M.s.* 'Mermaid', has a more compact habit and larger longer-lasting flowers. Height 15cm (6in), spread 30–45cm (1–1½ft).

Myriophyllum proserpinacoides (parrot's feather) is a vigorous plant that is unsuitable for small ponds. Although the long stems of blue-green feathery foliage that spread across the water's surface aren't particularly ornamental, it does have two immensely useful purposes. It is a good oxygenating plant and the feathery stems provide an ideal spawning ground for fish. It is susceptible to winter frost damage, so place the plant with its crown 15cm (6in) below the water's surface. As an extra precaution, cuttings can be rooted in late summer and kept in a frost-free place over winter. Height 15cm (6in), spread indefinite.

Pontederia cordata (pickerel weed) is a handsome, well-behaved plant for a small or large pond, forming a neat clump of

Above: Lysichitum camtschatcensis *bears shining, unusually-shaped flowers in early spring.*

Left: Zantedeschia *(Arum lilies) bear exotic white flowers in summer.*

glossy heart-shaped leaves and in late summer producing dense spikes of soft blue flowers borne on stems above the foliage. This is the best blue-flowered pond plant. It can be susceptible to frost damage, so place it with around 10cm (4in) of water over the crown of the plant. Height 75cm (2½ft), spread 45cm (1½ft).

Preslia cervina (American water mint) produces pretty bluish-mauve whorls of flowers in summer, and possesses narrow green leaves that give off a strong, pleasant, mint-like fragrance. This plant is also happy in marshy soil. For a small pond this is a much better plant to provide aromatic foliage than the more vigorous *Mentha aquatica* (water mint). Height and spread 45cm (1½ft).

Ranunculus lingua 'Grandiflora' (water buttercup or greater spearwort) is a vigorous and potentially invasive plant for larger ponds. It forms a clump of upright, lance-shaped, blue-green leaves and bears many large, bright yellow 'buttercup' flowers from late spring into summer. Height 60–90cm (2–3ft), spread 60cm (2ft). *R. flammula* is a more compact species but is less attractive. Ranunculus look good with other informal plants such as *Lythrum salicaria* (purple loosestrife) and *Menyanthes* (bog bean).

Sagittaria sagittifolia (arrowhead) forms a spreading clump of dark green, glossy, arrow-shaped leaves and bears small clusters of single white flowers in summer. Height and spread 90cm (3ft). This variety is vigorous and needs a large pond, but *S.s.* 'Flore Pleno' is less vigorous and can be grown in ponds of all sizes, though it does benefit from a sheltered site. Its double flowers are a mass of white petals. Height and spread 45cm (1½ft).

Saururus cernuus (swamp lily or lizard's tail) produces long pendulous spikes of fragrant white flowers in summer above green heart-shaped leaves that develop attractive tints in autumn. Height 23cm (9in), spread 30cm (1ft).

Veronica beccabunga (brooklime) is a useful spreading plant for concealing pond edges. It bears pretty, white-eyed, bright blue flowers through summer. Cut the entire plant hard back every spring to prevent it becoming straggly. Height 15–30cm (6–12in), spread 45cm (18in).

Zantedeschia aethiopica (arum lily) bears extremely handsome white flowers on stems above glossy, green, arrow-shaped leaves. Getting the best out of this plant can be tricky, however, as it is susceptible to frost and therefore needs to have its crown at least 15cm (6in) below the surface of the water. Alternatively overwinter it in a greenhouse. Height 60cm (2ft), spread 45–60cm (1½–2ft).

Marginal Ornamental Grasses and Rushes

Grasses and grass-like plants are perfect for growing in and around a pond. Their slender stems form elegant vertical clumps that make an ideal contrast to the bold lines of formal ponds, as well as blending and contrasting with other plants in an informal pond. Many have attractively coloured or variegated foliage that provides colour and interest from spring to autumn.

Several of the most vigorous rushes should be avoided unless you are planting a lake: they have little ornamental value for the garden pond, and their sharp growing tips can pierce a flexible liner or a thin pre-formed pond. Notable varieties to avoid are most *Typha* varieties – often incorrectly referred to as bulrushes, but which are in fact reed-maces – and *Sparganium ramosum* (bur-reed).

Acorus calamus 'Variegatus' (sweet flag) is an extremely handsome plant producing tall, sword-like, green leaves which are attractively striped with cream. In spring the leaves are also flushed with pink. Small brownish-green horn-shaped flowers are produced in summer, but the foliage is the main attraction of this plant. When crushed, the leaves give off a pleasantly pungent scent. Height 60–75cm (2–2½ft), spread 60cm (2ft). The green-leaved species, *Acorus calamus*, is much less ornamental than the variegated form.

Butomus umbellatus (flowering rush) is a striking plant for both flower and foliage interest. The triangular-shaped, green, rush-like leaves form a tall graceful clump of foliage, and in summer heads of pretty rose-pink flowers are borne on long stems above the foliage. Height 0.9–1.2m (3–4ft), spread 45cm (1½ft).

Cyperus longus (sweet galingale) forms large clumps of slender, dark green leaves. Heads of dark reddish-brown flowers are borne on tall stems in summer. This is a vigorous plant which is best in large ponds and is also happy in marshy ground on the very edge of the pond. However, it may not be hardy in severe winters and benefits from a mulch of straw. Height 1.2m (4ft), spread 60–90cm (2–3ft).

Glyceria maxima variegatus (manna grass) forms elegant clumps of leaves which are attractively striped with yellow, white and green, and in spring are delicately flushed with pink. This exceptionally invasive grass should definitely be grown in a container. Height 60cm (2ft), spread indefinite.

Juncus effusus spiralis (corkscrew rush) is the most ornamental of the juncus family – others don't have sufficient attraction to include in a garden pond. This variety has unusually contorted stems that grow in a corkscrew shape. Height 45cm (1½ft), spread 30cm (1ft).

Phalaris arundinacea var. *Picta* (gardener's garters) bears green-and-white-striped leaves, and is often seen growing happily in the garden border – too happily, in fact, as this easily-grown plant usually becomes an invasive nuisance. Growing it in a container in water solves the problem. Height 60cm (2ft), spread indefinite.

Scirpus tabernaemontani 'Zebrinus' (zebra rush) produces tall, slender, green leaves that are unusually banded horizontally with white. Occasionally plain green leaves are produced, which should be removed at once. *S. albescens* produces slender, pale yellow leaves that are vertically striped with slender bands of green. These varieties can become invasive and are best grown in containers. Height 0.9–1.2m (3–4ft), spread indefinite.

Typha minima (dwarf reed-mace) forms a neat clump of grassy foliage. In summer spikes of pale brown flowers are produced on short stems, followed by chunky, rich brown 'bulrush' seed heads. This variety is suitable for small ponds – all other varieties are too vigorous. Height 45cm (1½ft), spread 30cm (1ft).

OXYGENATING PLANTS

Oxygenating plants, which are also called submerged aquatics, are extremely useful in helping to maintain a healthy pond. They are mostly of little ornamental value as they form masses of submerged foliage, but they play an important functional role in the pond. These plants take up carbon dioxide which is exhaled by fish and other creatures, and produce life-giving oxygen as their name suggests. They also absorb mineral salts from the water. Unless these minerals are taken up by plants, microscopic green algae feed on them and rapidly turn pond water into a green soup.

Oxygenators are particularly useful if you plan to keep fish in your pond. As well as converting carbon dioxide, they also absorb other waste products from fish. The lush foliage is a useful source of fish food and provides an excellent spawning ground. Plant oxygenators at least two to four weeks before introducing fish to your pond so the plants have sufficient time to establish and withstand the robust attentions of the fish.

Most oxygenators are sold as bunches of unrooted cuttings, which need to be planted (see page 91). As a rough guide to the quantity required for a garden pond, allow one bunch of cuttings or one plant for every 0.2 square m (2 square ft) of pond surface area. They don't need to be equally distributed, so several bunches can be planted in one basket.

The majority of oxygenators require a sunny site in order to function properly, though a couple of varieties will grow in shade. The most vigorous varieties will need excess growth removed from time to time. As a general guide, trim strongly growing plants little and often, rather than pruning hard, which then gives algae a chance to establish. If it's not possible to trim the plants, use a rake to pull out excess growth, but take care not to remove too much at once. Leave the trimmings piled by the pond edge for a couple of days so that small creatures can return to the water.

Several plants are best avoided. *Tillaea recurva*, also known as *Crassula helmsii*, is an excellent oxygenator, but it is extremely vigorous and has started to over-run natural ponds and waterways. Another exceptionally vigorous plant is *Elodea canadensis* (Canadian pond weed). *Potamageton natans* is also very invasive.

Callitriche autumnalis (water starwort) is a very useful food plant for fish, which are fond of its pale green cress-like foliage. The leaves are also a haven for insect life.

Ceratophyllum (hornwort) is one of the most versatile oxygenators. It will grow in a shady as well as a sunny site, and can also grow in very deep water. The branched stems look like green bottle-brushes, and in summer some of the stems detach and become free-floating. There are two very similar species, *C. demersum* and *C. submersum*.

Fontinalis antipyretica (willow moss) is an excellent plant that will grow in sun or shade and is fairly slow-growing, but it does prefer to be in moving water and dislikes warm water. Its dark green feathery foliage looks particularly attractive when moving gently in the water's current. This plant is a particularly good spawning ground for fish.

Hottonia palustris (water violet) is a pretty plant that is one of the few flowering oxygenators. The flower stems rise from a mass of light green, feathery foliage and grow to around 15cm (6in) above the water's surface in early summer, bearing whorls of delicate lavender or white flowers. This plant prefers still water and a planting depth of around 30cm (1ft), but can sometimes be difficult to establish.

Lagarosiphon major (also sold under the name of *Elodea crispa*) is an excellent oxygenator that forms branching stems clothed with whorls of dark green foliage, but do be aware that it is also very vigorous once established and surplus growth will need to be removed regularly. If clearing excessive growth from your pond could be a problem, it may be best to avoid this variety.

Myriophyllum (water milfoil) is an attractive plant with feathery green foliage that provides an excellent spawning ground for fish. *M. spicatum* produces bronze-green foliage and bears small red-petalled flowers just above the water in summer. *M. verticillatum* has bright green foliage and small yellowish flowers in summer.

For details of *Myriophyllum proserpinacoides* see under 'Marginal Plants'.

BOG OR POOLSIDE PLANTS

Moisture loving plants growing in a bog garden are ideal partners for a pond or water feature. Although a bog garden can be created as a 'stand-alone' feature, it looks far more in keeping next to a pond, where the lush colourful bog plants make the perfect visual transition from garden to pond.

There is a rich variety of moisture-loving plants which can give your garden a wealth of colour and interest, with delicate flowers, coloured leaves and bold architectural foliage. The plants described here are principally herbaceous perennials, plus a number of ornamental grasses and ferns. Although most flourish in full sun, the majority of bog plants prefer a lightly shaded site. Larger plants such as shrubs are normally too substantial for most specially created bog gardens, though several suitable varieties are described in the following section on plants to associate with ponds.

Don't make the common mistake of trying to grow these moisture-loving plants in ordinary soil next to a pond without constructing a bog garden, unless your soil is naturally moist. Remember

Bog gardens look magnificent constructed on a larger scale where bold-foliaged plants, such as ligularias, ferns and hostas, can be planted in large clumps for maximum impact.

too that the soil must remain moist *all year* – plenty of gardeners have soils such as heavy clay that is disgustingly soggy through the winter months but becomes a cracked parched desert in the summer. A group of scorched, wilting bog plants is a pitiful sight in such a situation.

The vast majority of bog plants require soil that is constantly moist but not waterlogged. For the wettest part of the bog garden where it joins the pond, it's best to grow those bog plants, like mimulus, which are happy in such conditions, or choose from those marginals which thrive in marshy ground. Such marginals include caltha (kingcups), iris, lysichitum (skunk cabbage), *Lythrum salicaria* (purple loosestrife) and *Myosotis scorpioides* (water forget-me-not).

Astilbes are excellent bog garden plants that form clumps of attractive divided leaves and produce open fluffy spires of white, pink or red flowers in summer. Of the many different tall hybrids, some of the best include *Astilbe* 'Deutschland', pure white; *A.* 'Red Sentinel', dark red with reddish-green foliage; and *A.* 'Rheinland', bright pink. Height 60–90cm (2–3ft), spread 60cm (2ft). The smaller varieties are especially appealing. The best is *A. simplicifolia* 'Sprite' which produces feathery pale pink flowers and finely divided leaves. *A. chinensis* 'Pumila' bears dense spikes of deep rosy-pink flowers. Height and spread 45cm (1½ft).

Cardamine pratensis (cuckoo flower or lady's smock) is a charming little plant that produces clusters of delicate pale pink flowers on short stems in spring. It is excellent for the wildlife garden as it is a food plant for the orange tip butterfly. It looks lovely growing in grass at the water's edge, or in small drifts among kingcups. There is also a pretty double-flowered form, *C.p.* 'Flore Pleno'. Height 30cm (1ft), spread 15cm (6in).

Filipendula ulmaria 'Aurea' (golden meadowsweet), one of the few golden-leaved bog plants, creates a bright splash of gold that provides a good contrast for many other plants. White flowers are produced in summer, but I prefer to remove these to encourage fresh leaf growth. The leaves can be scorched by sun, so grow this plant in light shade. Height and spread 15–30cm (6–12in). There is also a green-and-white variegated form, but it is nowhere near as pretty.

Geum rivale (water avens) produces its warm coppery-pink flowers in early summer. These are borne on short stems above fresh green foliage, and nod delicately with their faces shyly turned towards the ground. The flower colour is set off well by variegated iris, and it goes superbly with the glossy leaves of *Calla palustris* (bog arum). Height 45cm (1½ft), spread 30cm (1ft).

Gunnera manicata (giant rhubarb) is a fantastic monster of a plant that provides a real talking-point, but such a massive plant needs a correspondingly large garden as it can easily achieve a height and spread of 1.8–2.4m (6–8ft). The enormous rhubarb-like leaves are produced on long stems, and large cones of greenish-yellow flowers are borne in summer. In winter protect the crown of the plant with straw in all but the mildest areas.

Hostas (plantain lilies) are magnificent foliage plants that no bog garden should be without. They form clumps of bold handsome leaves that look wonderful, whether several different varieties are grouped together or other plants of contrasting shape and colour, such as ornamental grasses, are planted alongside. There are many different varieties from which to choose. Some have large blue-green leaves up to 30cm (1ft) long, such as *Hosta* 'Krossa Regal' and *H. sieboldiana* 'Elegans'. Others produce green leaves which are variegated with gold or white, such as *H.* 'Shade Fanfare' and *H. crispula*, or just plain green leaves such as *H. lancifolia*. Stems of white or lilac flowers are borne in summer.

Slugs and snails adore hostas, so protect them from the moment the leaves start to appear. Surround the crowns with gravel and scatter slug bait if necessary. Use an aluminium sulphate-based slug killer which won't harm hedgehogs and other wildlife.

Ligularias are exceptionally handsome plants with large, bold leaves and tall stems of brightly coloured flowers. The reddish-green or dark green leaves emerge early in spring to form an attract-ive clump of fresh foliage. The flowers are borne on tall stems in summer. *Ligularia dentata* 'Desdemona' and 'Othello' produce bright orange daisy-like flowers. *L.* 'Gregynog Gold' bears bright yellow daisy-like flowers. Height and spread 60–120cm (2–4ft). This plant is another gourmet feast for snails, so take the same precautions as for hostas to avoid the leaves turning into lacy skeletons.

Lobelias for the bog garden bear no relation to the popular blue bedding lobelia. The moisture-loving varieties bear tall elegant stems of colourful flowers in mid- to late summer that rise from clustered rosettes of foliage. *Lobelia cardinalis* varieties bear flaming red flowers. Choose a variety such as *L.c.* 'Queen Victoria' which has striking reddish-purple foliage. This species can be killed by hard frosts, so a protective winter mulch of straw or similar material is advisable. *L. syphilitica* bears attractive clear blue flowers. *L. × vedrariensis* produces deep violet-purple ones. Height 90cm (3ft), spread 30cm (1ft).

Mimulus (monkey musk) varieties can be grown as marginals, but prefer very marshy soil. There is a number of varieties, most of which bear brightly coloured and spotted snapdragon-like flowers. They form sprawling carpets of fresh green foliage that is good for concealing pond edges. Several varieties are vigorous and should be planted with care, such as *Mimulus guttatus*, which bears bright yellow flowers splashed with red,

Left: Variegated grasses make perfect backdrops to other plants, such as this vivid orange mimulus.

Opposite: Pink primulas and a gold-leaved grass contrast with the reddish astilbe leaves.

and *M. cardinalis*, which produces red flowers. There are several varieties which aren't invasive, such as *M. ringens* with pale blue-mauve flowers, *M.* 'Whitecroft Scarlet' which bears bright red flowers, and *M.* 'Andean Nymph' with rose-pink flowers with creamy-yellow throats. Height and spread 30–60cm (1–2ft).

Peltiphyllum peltatum (umbrella plant) forms a spectacular mound of large wavy-edged leaves. But before the leaves appear, in spring thick reddish stems grow almost unnoticed from the bare soil, suddenly opening to produce a beautiful head of starry, pale pink flowers. Grow in sun or shade. Height and spread 90cm (3ft).

Moisture-loving primulas are exquisite plants, and at least one or two of the many available varieties should be included in every bog garden. *Primula denticulata* (drumstick primula) is one of the earliest plants to flower in spring, bearing rounded heads of white or mauve flowers. Height 30cm (1ft), spread 15cm (6in). The majority of varieties flower in early to mid-summer. Of the many candelabra primulas that bear colourful flowers clustered up their stems, choose from *P. bulleyana* (pale orange flowers), *P. japonica* 'Mount Fuji' (white), *P.j.* 'Miller's Crimson' (bright crimson), *P. pulverulenta* (deep crimson-purple) and *P. heladoxa* (deep yellow). Height 60cm (2ft), spread 45cm (18in). Plant several of these candelabra primulas together for a lovely display of colour against green or glaucous-leaved hostas.

P. florindae (giant Himalayan cowslip) is a particularly handsome plant. It forms a clump of bold foliage, from which arise tall stems topped with nodding, soft yellow flowers that are delicately scented. Height 90cm (3ft), spread 45cm (18in).

Rheum palmatum (ornamental rhubarb) is an imposing plant that produces large, lobed leaves up to 60cm (2ft) long. The form *R.p.* 'Atrosanguineum' is most handsome, bearing leaves that are reddish-purple when young and tall panicles of bright cerise-pink flowers in early summer. This plant is only for the larger bog garden as it can achieve a height and spread of 1.8m (6ft).

Rodgersias also have handsome foliage and are considerably smaller, suitable for most sizes of bog garden. They produce fans of ridged leaves and bear plumes of feathery flowers in summer. *Rodgersia aesculifolia* has bronze-green leaves and creamy flowers. *R. pinnata* 'Superba' has similarly coloured leaves and bears bright pink flowers. Height 60–90cm (2–3ft), spread 60cm (2ft).

Trollius (globe flowers) provide a bright splash of spring colour, with their rounded heads of orange or yellow flowers borne on stems above clumps of divided foliage. Good varieties include *Trollius* 'Earliest of All', with butter-yellow flowers; *T.* 'Orange Princess'

(orange-yellow); and *T.* 'Goldquelle', which bears warm orange flowers. Height 60cm (2ft), spread 45cm (18in).

Grasses and Ferns

Foliage plays a large role in the bog garden, both as a foil to other plants and as an attraction in its own right. Ferns are perfect waterside plants with their delicate, fresh green leaves, and the soft lines of ornamental grasses provide a striking contrast to other plants.

A number of the ornamental grasses listed as marginal plants are also happy in moist soil, and in addition there are a number of attractive small grasses. The *Carex* family is a pretty group of small colourful sedges that prefer moist soil. Good varieties include *C. morrowii* 'Evergold', which forms a neat clump of narrow leaves brightly edged with gold. *C. conica* 'Kansuge' is a recent introduction, with wide, arching, green leaves edged with gold. *C. stricta* 'Bowles Golden' forms an arching clump of leaves that turn bright yellow through summer. *C. siderostica* 'Variegata' bears wide cream-and-green variegated leaves. Height 30–60cm (1–2ft), spread 30cm (1ft).

Acorus gramineus 'Ogon' is a recent introduction, it forms clumps of slightly arching leaves which are prettily variegated with green and gold. Height and spread 30cm (1ft). *Imperator cylindrica* 'Red Baron' is another newer variety which is especially striking. It forms a clump of upright green leaves tipped at the ends with dark red, this colour spreading down the leaves as the season progresses. Height and spread 45cm (1½ft).

Two ferns make particularly good specimens for the bog garden. *Matteucia struthopteris* (ostrich fern) forms neat handsome 'shuttlecocks' of fresh green foliage, reaching 90cm (3ft) in height. It likes very boggy soil, but can become invasive. *Osmunda regalis* (royal fern) forms a massive, eye-catching specimen of delicate fronded foliage. Height up to 1.8m (6ft), spread 90cm (3ft).

FLOATING PLANTS

Floating aquatics, as their name suggests, float free on the surface of the water with their roots dangling beneath the surface to extract nutrients from the pond. They have a useful role to play in preventing the growth of algae by shading the water from excessive sunlight. Some varieties are particularly pretty with attractive flowers or foliage.

The floaters described here are non-invasive, but with a couple of exceptions are not frost-hardy. To keep floating aquatics over winter, remove a clump in early autumn and place in a bowl with a layer of soil on the bottom and filled with a few centimetres of water. Keep the bowl in a light frost-free place, at a minimum temperature of 10°C (50°F) – the windowsill of a cool room is ideal. Return the plants to the pond in spring once the danger of frosts has passed.

Floating Plants to Avoid

Lemna species (duckweeds) form carpeting mats of tiny fresh green leaves on the water's surface and can proliferate at an astonishing speed, especially in warm weather. Such carpeting plants can turn a pond into a dangerous hazard. If left to spread unrestricted, they will form a wall-to-wall carpet and completely conceal the water, so unwary visitors – especially children – tread on what appears to be a solid surface and go straight into the pond. These plants are also incredibly tenacious if you try to eradicate them. No matter how thoroughly you net and remove plant growth, some pieces always escape and start recolonizing your pond.

Another floating plant that can create a similar hazard is Azolla caroliniana (fairy moss), which forms a crinkled fern-like carpet of foliage that turns red in summer. This plant isn't quite so tenacious as duckweed, but can still form a dangerous wall-to-wall carpet. It is useful in a pond where algae is a persistent problem, as it rapidly takes up nutrients and shades the water, but it should be planted only in smaller garden ponds where there is easy access to clear surplus growth.

Eichornia crassipes (water hyacinth) is one of the loveliest and most exotic of all pond plants, though it does need a warm summer to flower successfully. It forms a rosette of rounded glossy foliage with leaf stalks swollen full of air, which keeps the plant afloat. Spikes of showy light blue flowers marked with gold, are produced in mid- to late summer. This plant doesn't tolerate any frost at all, so select some young plants to over-winter indoors. While nurturing this plant, it's amusing to think that it reaches pestilential proportions in tropical waterways.

Hydrocharis morsus-ranae (frogbit) forms rosettes of small, rounded, dark green leaves, rather like those of a miniature water lily, from which arise delightful little three-petalled flowers through summer. Frogbit can be left in the pond over winter, when it sinks to the bottom in autumn and reappears in spring. However, plants left in the pond can be slow to restart into growth in spring, so a handful kept indoors over winter will get off to a flying start.

Pistia stratiotes (water lettuce) forms rosettes of velvety lettuce-like leaves. It does produce greenish flowers but these are rather insignificant. This plant won't tolerate any frost at all, so take it indoors in early autumn. (If going to this trouble over a floating plant, water hyacinth is a lot more rewarding than water lettuce!)

Stratiotes aloides (water soldier) produces clusters of spiky foliage – the most apt and widely used description is that of a pineapple top floating on the water. It floats just beneath the surface, coming up only when it produces three-petalled white flowers in summer, after which it sinks to the bottom of the pond for the winter. It is completely hardy and can be left in the pond all year.

Above: Eichornia crassipes *(water hyacinth) floats on the water's surface, and produces its exotic blue, gold-centred flowers in hot, sunny conditions in summer.*

Opposite: Background planting can be used to considerable effect – this golden Acer japonicum *'Aureum' makes a superb backdrop to blue irises and pink primulas.*

Trapa natans (water chestnut) forms clusters of dark green serrated leaves which are kept afloat by their swollen air-filled stalks. Small white flowers are produced in summer. After an exceptionally hot summer the flowers are followed by large, black, shiny fruits that are edible as well as ornamental. This plant is actually an annual, but you can grow new plants by collecting the fruits and storing them indoors in water for placing in the pond the following spring.

PLANTS TO ASSOCIATE WITH PONDS

Apart from the planting in the actual pond and any bog garden planting, it's worth giving some thought to the surrounding plants that will be growing in ordinary garden soil. Unless your pond is formal and makes a feature all of its own, a pond as an isolated feature can look rather lonely and out of place if the surrounding planting consists only of, say, a few marigolds. To integrate your pond completely into the part of the garden which it occupies, the nearby planting needs to be in harmony with the pond itself. Depending on the type of pond edging, you may also want plants to trail over the edge of the water to soften and conceal its boundaries.

Plants that associate particularly well with water include those which have a gentle arching shape, bold or feathery foliage, or slender rustling stems. Such plants make a perfect backdrop to the pond and blend it in beautifully with the rest of the garden.

Specimen Plants and Small Trees

These larger plants are best sited at least a metre or two back from the pond, otherwise they can shed large quantities of leaves directly into the water. A small tree or specimen plant towards the back of your planting gives it a sense of grace

and proportion. If you've created a bog garden, some of these larger plants make a perfect backdrop, and contrast well with those growing in moist soil: tall slender clumps of bamboo with the massive rounded leaves of ligularias, for example.

There are several excellent small trees to plant near ponds. *Salix* varieties (willows) are natural partners for water; they grow happily in all soils except those which are light and dry. Avoid *Salix × chrysocoma*, the massive common 'weeping willow', for all except lakeside planting! Good weeping varieties that remain small trees include *S. purpurea* 'Pendula' and *S. caprea* 'Pendula'. Both form umbrella-shaped heads of weeping branches and are usually grafted at a height of 1.8m (6ft). Another good small willow is *S. integra* 'Hakuro Nishiki', which forms a slightly weeping head of branches clothed in attractive pink-and-white variegated leaves.

Aralia elata (Japanese angelica tree) forms a large shrub or small tree. It produces huge pinnate green leaves gathered together towards the tops of thick woody stems, and bears massive panicles of creamy-white flowers in late summer. If your budget allows, consider the pricy but spectacular *A. elata* 'Variegata' which bears stunning green-and-white variegated leaves. Aralias prefer sun or light shade. Height 1.5–3m (5–10ft).

Bamboos and ornamental grasses are perfect partners for ponds. They form thick clumps of slender leaves that rustle soporifically in the slightest breeze. *Arundinaria murieliae* forms a tall clump of canes that arch over to form a delicate fountain of foliage, as does *A. nitida*. *A.m.* 'Simba' is a newer and more compact form. Grow these in sun or partial shade. Height up to 3m (10ft).

Miscanthus sinensis varieties are handsome and useful ornamental grasses that form tall narrow clumps of slender leaves. *M.s.* 'Zebrinus' (zebra grass) is particularly eye-catching, with its leaf blades banded with yellow. Height 1.2–1.5m (4–5ft), spread 60cm (2ft).

Several shrubs have colourful stems that provide excellent winter colour, and the bright stems also reflect prettily in the water's surface. *Cornus* varieties (dogwoods) are useful shrubs with red, yellow or orange stems. Choose a variety such as *C. alba* 'Elegantissima', which has attractive variegated foliage for year-round interest. Dogwoods tolerate all except very dry soils, in sun or partial shade. Another good plant with coloured stems is *Salix alba* 'Britzensis', which produces glowing orange stems and prefers a moisture-retentive soil. Prune these shrubs hard in early spring to encourage plenty of new colourful shoots. Height and spread 1.2m (4ft).

There are several other handsome shrubby willows for waterside planting, which have very attractive foliage. *S. elaeagnos* clothes its reddish stems with beautiful, slender, silver-green leaves, while *S. exigua* produces silvery ones. Height 1.8–2.4m (6–8ft).

Smaller Shrubs, Perennials, Grasses and Ferns

Shrubs that form a mound of feathery foliage look wonderful next to water, and few are lovelier than *Acer palmatum* 'Dissectum' varieties (Japanese maples). These plants are a little fussy about their site; they need shelter from strong cold winds and require a moist but well-drained neutral or acid soil. There are several varieties with green, reddish or purple leaves. Height and spread 90cm (3ft).

Sambucus racemosa 'Tenuifolia' (cut-leaved elder) is similar in size and appearance to Japanese maples, but is tolerant of limy soil. It forms a mound of fresh green fern-like foliage. Height and spread 90cm (3ft).

Dwarf bamboos and grasses look lovely at the water's edge, particularly those with coloured foliage. *Arundinaria viridistriata* has leaves brightly striped with yellow and green. Those of *A. fortunei* are striped with white and green. Good green-leaved bamboos include *Shibataea kumasasa* with fresh green leaves. Height 60–120cm (2–4ft).

Hakonochloa macra 'Aureola' (Japanese golden grass) forms cascading clumps of leaves which are brilliantly striped with gold. *Molinia caerulea* 'Variegata' forms neat clumps of leaves striped with green and cream. As a contrast, grow the unusual *Ophiopogon planiscapus nigrescens* (Japanese black grass), which forms little spidery clumps of narrow black leaves.

Height and spread from 15cm (6in) to 60cm (2ft).

A number of herbaceous perennials look wonderful associated with water. Many have a slightly spreading habit that makes them ideal for concealing or softening the edges of a pond.

Ajuga (bugle) is an excellent ground-covering plant that forms mats of colourful foliage – green, variegated or purple – from which arise short stems of blue flowers in spring. Height 15cm (6in), spread 60cm (2ft). *Alchemilla mollis* (lady's mantle) forms a spreading clump of lovely, scalloped, fresh green leaves that hold dew in tiny quicksilver pearls. A mass of feathery, bright yellow-green flowers is produced in early summer. This plant can seed itself everywhere, so cut off the heads immediately after flowering to prevent this happening. Height and spread 45cm (1½ft).

Dicentra eximia varieties form low mounds of ferny foliage and bear locket-like flowers on short stems in late spring. White-, pale-pink-, and dark-pink-flowered varieties are available. Height and spread 30cm (1ft). *Lysimachia nummularia* (creeping jenny) is a mat-forming plant that grows roots on each spreading stem to form a green carpet studded with bright gold flowers in summer. *L.n.* 'Aurea' is even prettier, with soft gold foliage. Height 5cm (2in), spread 45cm (1½ft).

Other good plants to consider include *Aruncus* 'Kneiffii', epimediums, hemerocallis, heucheras, *Iris foetidissima*, lamiums and *Vinca minor* (lesser periwinkle).

PROBLEMS AND MAINTENANCE

After your water feature has been completed, virtually all you need to do is to sit back and enjoy the results of your work. However, there are a few essential maintenance jobs that make an enormous difference to the health and appearance of your pond or water feature.

By following guidelines on pond siting, construction and planting, you should greatly reduce the chances of any pond problems. Nonetheless several common problems can occur, especially with new ponds. These and how to tackle them are covered in the second half of this chapter.

Spring and Early Summer Pond Maintenance

Overgrown plants are the main area needing maintenance in spring, unless your pond has become full of debris.

Cleaning

Spring is the best time to empty and clean a pond, but don't be tempted to do this too often or you'll upset the pond's natural balance. As an approximate guide, small ponds should be cleaned out totally only every five years and large ponds every ten

This is an established pond that needs little maintenance, though it should be netted in autumn to catch the purple acer leaves.

years. The exception is if your pond is obviously polluted, with black, milky or foul-smelling water, in which case it will need cleaning immediately.

To clean out a pond, first remove the water by bailing or siphoning it into a lower part of the garden, running it through a net to catch creatures such as tadpoles. Put these, the fish and the plants into buckets of water while work is being carried out. Then use a stiff brush and clean water to scrub the inside of the pond, taking care not to stand in the pond unless it is made of concrete. Empty the dirty dregs of water out before refilling with fresh water.

Plants

As well as being the ideal period for introducing new plants to the pond, spring/early summer is also the best time of year for attending to established plants. Rejuvenate those which have formed large congested clumps by lifting and dividing their rootstocks. The length of time before this becomes necessary varies according to the vigour of the plant. As a general guide for water lilies, vigorous varieties need dividing after three years and dwarf varieties after around five years. Most marginal plants benefit from division after about three years.

First gather all the necessary materials so that the plants will be out of the water for as short a time as possible – remember to keep them moist at all times. In addition to the planting materials detailed on page 90, you will need a sharp knife for dividing water lilies and two garden forks for dividing big clumps of marginals. A large sheet of polythene spread next to the pond makes a good work surface, keeping your lawn or paving free of debris and enabling pond creatures to be easily returned to the water.

Dividing a marginal plant is very similar to dividing a herbaceous perennial. Take the plant out of its container, insert the two garden forks back to back in the plant, then lever the forks apart to split the clump in two. Depending on the size of the original plant, this process can be repeated several times to result in smaller clumps which can be replanted as described on page 90. The old centre of the plant should be discarded.

Dividing a water lily. Take the plant out of its container and wash off the soil so that the rootstock is clearly visible. This will consist of a main rootstock with smaller rootstocks or sideshoots. Using a sharp knife, remove the sideshoots where they join the main stem, and dust the cut surface with sulphur to help prevent infection. Replant the sideshoots and discard the old rootstock.

Oxygenating plants can produce lots of vigorous growth that needs to be reduced occasionally. Do this by cutting off surplus growth if accessible, or by using a garden rake to pull out excessive growth. Leave this surplus weed piled by the water's edge for a couple of days to enable pond creatures such as small snails to make their way back in.

Feeding of aquatic and marginal plants should be carried out in spring using sachets or tablets of special slow-release aquatic plant fertilizer. Simply push one sachet into the soil of each plant container: one application should last the whole season. Don't worry about oxygenating and floating plants as they extract sufficient nutrients from the water. Never use ordinary garden fertilizers in the pond – these would create enormous problems by releasing massive amounts of nutrients into the water, enabling algae to thrive.

Loss of Water through Evaporation

During hot weather the water level may need topping up. Rain water from a water butt is best; otherwise use tap water added little and often, which disturbs the balance of the pond less than if it is added in large quantities.

Fish Feeding

Fish live off their reserves in winter, but in spring start feeding them a little at a time as the weather warms up and increase feeding gradually through spring until they are being fed daily. As a guide to the amount required, fish should eat all the food within half an hour – if there is any left after that time, reduce the quantity, because uneaten food releases nutrients into the water and again will encourage algae to proliferate.

Autumn and Winter Pond Maintenance

Keeping the pond clear of fallen leaves is important, as they otherwise accumulate and decompose over winter, giving off gases that are toxic to fish and other wildlife. A certain amount of waste will have accumulated through the year, so first use a net or scoop to dredge as much debris as possible from the base of the pool. Then stretch a fine mesh net or wire netting over the pond to collect fallen leaves, which can be periodically removed to the compost heap.

Cut off leaves of aquatic plants as they die back from early autumn onwards. With those marginal plants that have hollow stems, take care not to cut below water level or plants can actually 'drown'. Remove surplus oxygenating plant growth as described under 'Spring/Early Summer Maintenance'. Take out floating plants such as water hyacinth which are not frost-hardy, and over-winter indoors as described on page 110.

Fish Feeding

Fish should receive decreasing amounts of food as the temperature drops in autumn, and should not be fed at all over winter as they live off their reserves.

Pumps

Pumps not in use over winter should be removed, cleaned in fresh water to flush out sediment and stored according to the manufacturer's instructions. Pumps that

Above: Water lilies can form dense clumps of leaves that need to be thinned occasionally.

Opposite: Clean wooden decking occasionally to stop it becoming slippery.

remain in the pond should be at least 45cm (18in) deep so that they don't become frozen, and should be run fortnightly for a short time to prevent silt or scale build-up. External pumps remaining in place should be drained and insulated.

Ice

Ice forming a solid layer on the pond for more than a day or two allows toxic gases to build up underneath. A small hole should be made in the ice to allow oxygen in and gases out. Never break ice with a sharp blow – this can concuss or kill the pond's inhabitants. Instead stand a pan of boiling water on the ice to melt a hole

through it gradually, or float a ball in the water that can be removed to leave a hole. If you have a pump that has been removed for the winter, you can use the wiring set-up to install a pond heater – a tubular electrical element encased in polystyrene – to keep a small area permanently ice-free.

Snow lying on the ice for more than a couple of days should be swept off to allow light to reach the pond.

Potential Pond Problems

Once established, a properly designed and planted pond should rarely be subject to problems.

Green Water

Green water is a frequent occurrence, especially with newly filled ponds. The green colour is caused by millions of microscopic algae which thrive on the mineral salts that occur naturally in water. Tap water is particularly rich in mineral salts, hence this rapid greening of newly filled ponds. The easiest mistake is to drain the 'dirty' water away and refill the pond, because the fresh water will simply turn green again very shortly. The only ways to resolve the problem permanently are by planting a variety of aquatic plants to create a balanced environment in the pond, as described in detail on page 86, or by installing a filter system in conjunction with a pump (see page 70).

Green water often occurs in established ponds in spring. Here the problem is usually temporary, as the aquatic plants are only just coming into growth and are not yet fully functioning. The problem is usually resolved once plants are growing strongly. Over-feeding of fish is another common cause of algal growth – see the guidelines on page 119.

Blanketweed

Blanketweed is a form of algae that can be a particular nuisance. It grows in long thin strands and can form clumps like green cotton wool. Again the best way of solving the problem is by creating a natural balance with plants, but it may be necessary to remove blanketweed regularly, by twirling it round a stick or just pulling it out by hand.

Recent research has shown that small bundles of barley straw submerged in a pond actually control blanketweed and other algae, though the reasons are not yet fully known. Further investigation is currently being carried out.

Another device that has been found to reduce blanketweed is a magnetic water treatment that is used in conjunction with a filter and an ultra-violet clarifier system, though it does have some drawbacks (see page 71).

Both blanketweed and other algae can be combated with chemical algicide, but this is really a short-term treatment of the symptom rather than a cure. If you use one, take great care to follow the manufacturer's instructions, and remove large amounts of dead algae as soon as possible.

Snails and Mussels

Snails and mussels are natural scavengers that help remove algae and pond debris, but they should be introduced with care. Some types of snail are just as happy tucking into treasured ornamental plants, and for this reason only the ramshorn snail can be recommended.

Swan mussels should be introduced only to large ponds that already contain a good layer of debris on the floor in which they can live. If the pond environment is unsuitable, the mussels will die and cause considerable water pollution.

Garden Fertilizers and Manure

Use garden fertilizers and manure with care near a pond, as rain can wash them into the pond from the surrounding soil. This creates nutrient-rich water and will result in a proliferation of green algae. Some fertilizers are also toxic to fish.

Cloudy Water

Fish stirring up sediment in the pond may cause the water to become cloudy. This can be prevented by covering the base of the pond and the tops of plant containers with a layer of washed pea gravel. Another cause of cloudy water is soil washing in from higher ground that surrounds the pond. This is a basic design flaw which can be corrected only by a physical barrier of stones or other material to prevent soil entering the pond.

Repairing Leaky Ponds

Leaks, as opposed to natural evaporation, soon become apparent when the water level of a pond quickly falls and stops at the level of the leak. Effective repairs can be carried out on some types of pond, though cheaper liners often cannot be repaired successfully.

Flexible Liners

You can patch flexible pond liners using repair kits of special self-adhesive material – rather like repairing a bicycle inner tube. First drain the pond and clean thoroughly around the damaged area with a brush and water. Leave to dry, then use sandpaper to roughen the surface lightly. Cut a patch of repair material large enough to allow a good overlap, place over the puncture and press firmly. Leave for at least twenty-four hours before refilling the pond.

Cheaper types of liner such as polythene or PVC have a short life and often aren't worth repairing, particularly if the liner begins to disintegrate around the edge of the pond where it has been exposed to sunlight.

Concrete Ponds

A concrete pond can be repaired if there are only a couple of cracks. After draining the pond, chisel out the crack to a V-shape at least 2.5cm (1in) deeper than the original crack, and chip the surface of the surrounding area. Mix sufficient concrete, adding a waterproofing compound, then fill the crack and smooth it over. Treat with a sealing compound. (See Project 3: Making a Concrete Pond for details on compounds.)

Old concrete ponds that are suffering only from hairline cracks can sometimes be resealed with a coat of waterproofing paint, which is a form of liquid plastic. Severely damaged concrete ponds can be relined with a flexible liner to seal the existing cavity.

If all else fails, you can always turn a perpetually leaking pond into an attractive bog garden!

Plant Pests and Diseases

Fortunately plant pests are few, which is just as well because chemical sprays should never be used in or around a pond. Fish and pond creatures are a considerable help in controlling pests too.

Aphids

Aphids can infest the leaves and flowers of water lilies and other pond plants. To get rid of them, simply weigh down the plant growth under water for twenty-four hours, whereupon pond creatures will make a meal of the aphids.

Water Lily Beetle

Water lily beetle is a small brown beetle that lays its eggs in early summer. These hatch into yellow-bellied black grubs that eat the leaves, which then die off. Remove and destroy affected leaves, and hose the remaining foliage with a strong jet of water to dislodge grubs. The adult beetle hibernates in the dead stems of marginal plants, so it helps to remove these in autumn.

Water Lily Leaf Spot

Water lily leaf spot tends to be a problem only during long spells of damp warm weather. Spots appear on the leaves and increase in size, eventually rotting and forming holes. Control by removing and destroying infected leaves.

Water Lily Crown Rot

Comparatively little is known as yet about water lily crown rot; it causes the entire plant, including the crown, to die and rot. The disease only appears to spread when many plants are in close proximity, and lilies rarely succumb once established in a pond. If you have purchased a lily that dies *completely* within several weeks, take it back to your supplier.

Fish Predators

There are two main predators that can seriously deplete fish levels in garden ponds:

Herons

Herons tend to be pests only if you keep fish, and a determined heron can be a formidable opponent. Several methods can be employed to help deter them. These massive birds land near the pond and walk the few steps to its edge, so a single wire stretched on cones around the pond at a height of around 15cm (6in) can catch the bird's legs and scare it off. An artificial heron by the pond is said to convince passing herons that competition is already there, though in truth the heron would have to be suffering severe eyesight problems for this method to work. The only sure-fire protection is to cover your pond permanently with a net.

Cats

Cats often try to catch fish. Constructing a pond edge with an overhang of at least 5cm (2in) gives fish somewhere to shelter, as do water lilies with their large leaves. If the pond surroundings allow, a scattering of prickly prunings such as roses, holly or berberis can deter cats. A similar deterrent can be purchased in the form of plastic mesh with short upright spikes.

USEFUL ADDRESSES

Pumps, filters & other sundries.

Bradshaws
Freepost 56
Nicolson Link
Clifton Moor
York YO1 1SS

Tel: 0904 691169

Pond liners.

CPS Aquatic
Freepost
Langford
Biggleswade
Beds. SG18 9GP

Tel: 0462 700507

Moisture-loving plants, including many less usual varieties.

Rowden Gardens
Brentor
Tavistock
Devon PL19 0NG

Tel: 0822 810275

Wide range of water garden products and plants.

Stapeley Water Gardens Ltd.
London Road
Stapeley, Nantwich
Cheshire CW5 7LH

Tel: 0270 621811

Range of pond liners (not just butyl) & sundries.

Wight Butyl Liners Ltd.
Market Square
St Neots
Cambs. PE19 2BG

Tel: 0480 403477

Water lilies & other aquatic plants.

Wychwood Carp Farm
Farnham Road
Odiham
Nr Basingstoke
Hampshire RG25 1HS

Tel: 0256 702800

OTHER *GARDENERS' WORLD* TITLES AVAILABLE FROM THE BBC

Gardeners' World
PERFECT PLANTS FOR PROBLEM PLACES
by Gay Search

Gardeners' World
VEGETABLES FOR SMALL GARDENS
by Lynda Brown

Gardeners' World
PLANTS FOR SMALL GARDENS
by Sue Fisher

Gardeners' World
BOOK OF CONTAINER GARDENING
by Anne Swithinbank

Gardeners' World
BOOK OF HOUSEPLANTS
by Anne Swithinbank

Gardeners' World
BOOK OF BULBS
by Sue Phillips

INDEX

Page numbers in *italic* refer to the illustrations